BACK OFF, ASSASSIN!

NEW & SELECTED POEMS

Printed in Canada

Library and Archives Canada Cataloguing in Publication

Smith, Jim, 1951-
Back off, assassin! : new and selected poems / Jim Smith.

Poems.
ISBN 978-1-894469-45-6

I. Title.

PS8637.M564B34 2009 C811'.54 C2009-905203-2

Editor for the Press: Stuart Ross
Cover Design: Mansfield Creative
Cover Image: From a 1920 ROSTA poster by Vladimir Mayakovsky.
(Thanks to Staci Patten for enhancing the image.)
Author Photo: Stuart Ross
Typesetting: Stuart Ross

The publication of *Back Off, Assassin! New & Selected Poems*
has been generously supported by
The Canada Council for the Arts and
The Ontario Arts Council.

ONTARIO ARTS COUNCIL
CONSEIL DES ARTS DE L'ONTARIO

Canada Council for the Arts
Conseil des Arts du Canada

Mansfield Press Inc.
25 Mansfield Avenue, Toronto, Ontario, Canada M6J 2A9
Publisher: Denis De Klerck
www.mansfieldpress.net

BACK OFF, ASSASSIN!
NEW & SELECTED POEMS

JIM SMITH

Mansfield Press

for Jo-Anne

CONTENTS

Introduction

The 1980s were a fertile and exciting time for the Toronto small press movement. The Toronto Small Press Book Fair was launched; Kevin Connolly was publishing his Pink Dog chapbooks; Lillian Necakov was producing visual and written work through her Surrealist Poets' Gardening Assoc.; Underwhich Editions was the foremost purveyor of experimental literature in Canada; half a dozen writers were selling their chapbooks out on Yonge Street, led by fiction writer Crad Kilodney and poet Don Garner. Meanwhile, *WHAT!* magazine was the scene's standard-bearer, while my own *Mondo Hunkamooga* was its watchdog. Daniel Jones was publishing books that began with his own denunciations of those very books. jwcurry was rubber-stamping one-cent publications almost daily. Over at Coach House Press, Stan Bevington was experimenting with dot-matrix portfolios of works by Michael Ondaatje and Victor Coleman. Maggie Helwig was making wonderfully grotty chapbooks by herself and her pals through Lowlife Publishing. bpNichol was creating Pong-like visual poems on some prehistoric Apple computer. And the internet was still merely a footnote at that time, while the printed page was exploding.

Amidst it all, there was this guy named Jim Smith, who was frenetically inspiring, challenging, and annoying us.

I can't recall exactly how I came to know Jim or his work. But it was a meeting, in the early 1980s, that changed my own writing and my own life. What astonished me about Jim's poetry was its directness, its courage, and its outrageousness. Newspaper headlines meeting surrealism head-on. Confession meeting crime. I hadn't ever met poetry like his, or anyone like him. All of this translated, too, to Jim's readings: at a *WHAT!* event, he had himself tied to a chair and interrogated himself, throwing his bound body all over the stage; at the Axletree Coffeehouse, he burned his own book along with Ronald Reagan's dick—well, a foil-wrapped chunk of sausage standing in for it, anyway (Jim made sure to offer an unburned copy of his book to the firefighters who soon arrived); he smashed bottles, denounced his dying father, and sang along to recordings of himself singing along to Stan Rogers. At the ArtCulture Resource Centre, Jim gave a three-hour reading where the introductions were about four times longer than the texts.

When Jim abruptly left the poetry world in the late 1990s, leaping into the cauldron of law school so he'd never have to work another crappy job again, Canadian poetry seemed to have forever lost one of its most energetic, unique, and essential voices. I was pissed off. It was an era when onetime small pressers were hiring agents, and new poets were skipping the sacred chapbook stage and grovelling to be published by the cream of the literary presses. Community was being sacrificed for career-building. We needed Jim, and he'd sold out ... to the law.

But he couldn't stay away. A decade later, Jim began dipping his toes tentatively into poetry again, and then he just dove right in. The work he has produced since his hiatus is the natural continuation of what came before, though the best of this new writing is even stronger. In the 2000s, politics still drives him, whether it's the politics of Canada, the imperial force to the south, or Jim's personal politics. And new characters have entered his body of work: joining Alexander Graham Bell, Leonel Rugama, and Arnold Schwarzenegger are bpNichol, Salvador Allende, and a dog named Nibbles.

When considering the format this book would assume, I was inspired by Ron Padgett's *New & Selected Poems* from 1995. Ron's book wasn't chronological, and the new and the selected were blended; what emerged was simply a new book by Ron Padgett. Because Jim's writing in *Back Off, Assassin! New & Selected Poems* will be his introduction to so many readers, we decided to emulate the Padgett formula. This way, the separate decades since Jim began publishing disappear, and the various invasions, coups, and revolutions—personal and otherwise—cease to be a chronology: as in some hallucinatory Philip K. Dick novel, everything happens at once. I'm just guessing, but I think that might make this book more like Jim's brain.

Stuart Ross
July 2009

There is a cyclone fence between
ourselves and the slaughter and behind it
we hover in a calm protected world like
netted fish, exactly like netted fish.
It is either the beginning or the end
of the world, and the choice is ourselves
or nothing.

Carolyn Forché
From "Ourselves or Nothing"

Assassin Take One

I keep Gene Day in a file folder in the basement.

My mother is a pile of letters and two casserole dishes on top of a bookshelf.

Arnie is in an urn waiting to be mixed with mine plus a sprinkle in the backyard he lay in.

Merril is some smudged pix, and a book by her granddaughter that mentions me once.

Sad brother Kim is his "K" keychain and a Cream disc I'll never ask why he had.

bp is one deadication, two anecdotes, a warm feeling, the rest appropriated years ago.

Richard Swanton our union friend and precocious AIDS dier, I have his key to our Robarts staff room.

These bits are basement tenants
Who've never paid a cent in rent.

Many of us have little piles of stuff.
Many have not a fucking thing.

Me, I've tried to forget myself
One dimension at a time.
I'm down to four now
So back off, assassin,
I'm shitting trinkets as fast as I can.

The Griping Forest

The forest has another gripe, see?
Because I lost its slippers.
They got folded, hopped right out
Into a clearing, caught cold,
Were hospitalized.

I valiantly tried to save them with Bloody Slim
Who wrote the book on slipperology.

But over vindaloo later, I told the whole story, how
Their livers went for a hundred bills to a local dealer.

bp

bp was on fire
& as we rolled him round the room
to put him out, each of us
threw ourselves on the pile
But he just blazed up
He consumed us all
& when they found us they
had to wrap what was left
in foil.

Anger

Yes, it is true. In anger
I held a glass in my hand as
I smashed that hand down on the hardwood table.
I felt nothing at the time.
Then only revulsion at the weakness of the flesh
that allowed blood to flow
indiscriminately.
Several piercing wounds
connected my hidden interior flesh to the air
polluted by the seed of my oppressors.

Blood flowed along my lifeline and dripped,
leaving a trail—that is how you found me
here in the bathroom, crying out
that I should not be spared the soft nausea
of knowing I hurt myself, knowing
there is a connection I failed to make
in the second of descent.

What caused me to do this? I do not really know.
It is probably there in your psychology books
but the person there is not me,
as I am not this person whose stomach is so weak
and who is so distant from himself that he is repulsed
by a wound in his own body.
What if I had been shot?
Could I lack so much control
that I would die?
My anger has driven me to this:
I do not know.

The trail of blood through living room
does not lead me to my other victims,
it only leads me to myself,
who has changed and surprised himself so much
he does not know what to say that he is.

I am here, there is salt in my mouth,
my nose is full, my stomach churns.

I want to look into the second that the glass
began moving downward,
the second I stood between
aggressor and victim,
somewhere beyond law.

Les Anges du Péché

The typewriter is broken,
It is moving of its own accord
Across the page.
It is hurling insults at me—
Why not type all the time, it challenges.
You don't get the full use out of me,
It declares. I have rights too.
It says it has seen me typing on the sly
With other type-
Writers.

I can't stand up to that sort of treatment,
So I type out I'm sorry
For whatever it is that made you so angry,
How about if we go away together,
Just the two of us, somewhere,
And work this out, make it the way it used to be
Between us.
But there is only silence.
Finally I look under the cover, and discover
A burnt smell,
The typewriter has shorted out.
I wonder what to do, and can think of nothing else,
So I call the hospital,
But the phone won't work,
It keeps crying softly,
In some foreign tongue.

Crinoid Hill

"another Hungry Hollow poem"
—bpNichol

I.

Its roots were feet buried in the sand,
its eyes a 360-degree panoply.
"What is the biggest of all creatures?" it said.

Driving back into the city
a giant trilobite strapped across the hood.
The story is that all the men spent their money
in the usual way, the families went hungry,
died and became fossils—
hence, hungry hollow.

Out here fresh land exposed,
easily eroded.   As belief.
As belied by experience.

Richard points out that you always miss the Hungry Hollow Road,
it is always necessary to ask directions.
They become necessary as we mark the increasing sophistication
of the rising levels.
At the bottom is confusion,
the exact locus of the belly
mixed and scrambled
with spatial dislocation.

We can't because of the river, it says.
Follow the long *i* of the bridge.
One of the usual pursuits of the men was sex—
clusterfuck, a word for group sex.

It echoes in the car
as the warning is received:
"Objects in mirror are closer than they appear," it says.

"How came you here?" it says,
have we passed over something,
bridged it, has something
escaped.
Is that the sound of something sliding to the bottom of the heap?
Two women climb into the cab of the truck—
they are off to have sex with men
who have forgotten how to feed their families.

2.

The population of any urban centre is an abstract number.
An approximation.
Each urban centre enfolds certain historic sites.
Turn to see
objects in the mirror
getting closer.
Suddenly we are surrounded on the highway by a convoy
of dilapidated buses with wraparound curtains.
The next sign predicts that 8 will become both 7 and 9
at the next juncture.
The uncertainty principle. The next time
we look, the buses have turned off to highway 2
which is withered from disuse.
They are travelling backward in time to the 1950s
before the 401.
One will stop in Kingston
and disgorge a waitress and a fat man with diseases
and me wrapped in a blanket.

3.

A new thought is trapped
in the cloverleaf.
I undergo the second warning: nausea—
the eye's disjuncture.
There is too much passing by outside to focus on the text.
My inner ear is like a cloverleaf.

I undergo the synaesthesia of pre-vomit.
There is the taste of breastmilk
in the back of my throat.
In one second
the dense physical
rise ejects thought.

My throat is the first part
to realize the falsity—
I am not going to throw up.
Something has been lost—
the peristaltic evacuation of the mind
has left a peace behind.

The new thought, trapped,
undergoes the squeeze of time
and is fossilized.

We go ahead to pick it up.

4.

We slide into the groove of hill, drive deep
into the lower Devonian,
an area of pure limestone
(like Kingston)

SOUTH______________here_______________NORTH
it flattens out

and there is a geography to the head
revealed in landscape:

in the mirror objects
look closer (active tense)
than (comparative)
they are (copulative tense).

On the radio it said
oh baby just you shut your mouth
she said
shhhhh
shhhhh
said
shhhhh
the radio it said.

The mind is like this
drive deep into me, baby, the hill said
I am a furrow
plant your seed well
so as to avert hunger.

5.

My brain travels about five feet
above surface
word spout
a gleam above surface.
A sign.
Enter Shakespeare, Ontario—and a low frame house

the entire lawn studded with Sylvester, Tweety Pie, Porky Pig
composed of planes of wood, coloured like life, their legs
pumping in the wind, whoooooooooooooof, the sign
lawn ornaments, but it is all a sign, Richard says.
The little guy would like one of them, and I know
he means me.

Two hundred representations
all working hard
running on the spot,
something that has crawled out of the imagination,
got up and walked.
The Stratford Mall says c'mon in—
we've got movies
of the past.
See fossils in action.

In 31 years my brain has grown only
four feet from its starting position.

For a moment
I thought I saw a puddy cat.
Then it was the past.

I did, I did, it said.

6.

The Mall: a later formation
a different period
complexity
the scale changes
"I thought I saw some rigid people there," Richard says.

"You did, you did," it says.

7.

Ah nature ah stress
ahhhhhhhhhh lunch:
a pulling-away of the meat from the bone
with the teeth.

A *slurrrrrrup* at the pit
of the stomach

and how we feel when done.
A silent time, the factory
in the area seldom travelled,
bulging with the product
of our times.

So organic. So organistic—
just as the lake swallows memory:

putting my hand in and I see how it bends
unnaturally, I pull out in fear
to see if I am alright:

the diffraction of different densities:

the distraction of memory
memory which is having me for lunch
every day of my life.

8.

"This reminds me of the old days," it says
"you go for 40 miles
and you are there."
As the radio tells us
there are no aliens here

we pass an outcrop of phalli
on the left
they pull together
tightening up into funk.

I really like the opening riff
into the past.

"You got me, you really got me," it says
there are tanks under pressure
below the farm phalli
"we are almost there," it says
"open your mouth," it says
ahhhhhhhhh—the past
"we are now in the middle Devonian era,"
we are almost always
someplace
like this
resisting music or
swallowing that which we do not
really understand.

The sun is hot,
we have still not identified
the hungry hollow
within
the image of ourselves
shifting,
just then a common mirage ahead
water on the road
"open your mouth," it says
always slightly ahead.

As the sound of running water pours forth
from the radio
it is all around us
we are swimming through it.

I find I am hungrier than ever
"we must be getting nearer," the hunger says
"what we are looking for."

9.

I suddenly think: "we are actually running
on fossil fuels," as a sign says:

FOR THOSE WHO DIED IN THIS COUNTRY

We cross the river.
I blink my eyes
over and over: this layering of vision
becomes heavier and presses down
on the image of the river
until it too is captured in the mind.
There are lesser and greater complex forms.
There are all those who died
in this country
in the scree
at the bottom of the layered
years.
"Anywhere along here is OK," it says,
and we pull up into the perfect circle
of dilapidated buses,
we all pile out and join Sylvester, Tweety,
the whole gang,
even babies in blue blankets,
we are digging
through the earth's complex layers,
each striving to find the perfect fossil
of the mother who died of hunger.

“I’ll remember this
for next time,” I say

“You will, you will.”

Indie Act

Long unhinged
From the machinations
Of the catholics
I announce to you right now, today:
I have my own faith.
It is a small, new country
That ends just past my nose.

This is one of the perks
Of being 57, the right
To flee any church so eager
To put me underground.

I'm not nuts about it, sure,
Not like if a flower gave me a nice smell
When it touched my body.

Sort of delirious, enough
To make a butterfly convulse
When it appears crowned
With an apparatus
That resembles my soul.

May the Fifth International forgive me.

Here, in Toronto, this whatever
Of November, current year,

Wildly aware of what needs doing!

After "Acta de Independencia" by Nicanor Parra

Your Big Day

You spread a map on the floor, stride from Chile to Paris to Chicago to Toronto to New York to Chile. Big steps. Small soldiers tickle your feet. Skeletons climb down out of corners and clamber over the soldiers. Pits fill with brass casings hot from tiny guns. A tank grinds up. You step on it. You marry three times. A national anthem plays until it is overthrown. A poet is buried on Isla Negra. You paint a chrome-yellow sun on the ceiling. It goes nova. Everything is incinerated, but for Nicanor Parra, who floats alone in space. Hi, Nicanor. We love you.

A Final Vision

Well, I picked the phone up & instead of the hum that says OK go ahead & dial, there were barnyard noises. I'm a resourceful person, & it took me only a few minutes to disassemble the black box. Inside, instead of coils & wires, there was a tiny & perfect pastoral paradise, glint of sun on tanned thighs, the smell of animal flesh, & the slow grunting of vegetables up through the loam; even the woodsmoke fresh & pure. I marvelled at how this could be. Reverently, I reassembled the casing. Jealously, I guard my secret, knowing someday the right connection will be made & I will meet you down in there.

For now, I feel a secret happiness at every incongruous noise over & under, behind & around your voice on the phone. When I am in love, I think you might already be there & only waiting there for me to smarten up, drop my body like work clothes & let the real me, tiny & perfect & naked, crawl out my ear & down into the receiver, finally arriving in the garden, just as the sun rises.

To Roque Dalton in El Salvador—Letter One

We are both still alive. Yet it is taken for granted that our mail is opened by others, read by others and disposed of. Does it make you want to scream, as I do? After all, this is the throat of the Americas, even if they treat it like the toilet's bowl. Surveillance—always to be under surveillance. How do we come to cope with it? Every day someone we know is picked up and taken to the edge of the city, where the garbage builds up in heaps, and they are hacked into pieces, or kicked into the other world (wherever that might be), and usually their hands are cut off—do you ever sit in the heat and imagine what it actually feels like to have a machete descend through the flesh and the muscle and the tendon and finally the bone and through flesh again—and there they lie until some kid comes along and watches the flies. My vision of those flies is a horde of little green *guardia*, buzzing and attacking and consuming and laying their evil eggs. In someone we know. Over and over and over again, every day that we live.

This we must endure, the certainty there will be a day when it's us on the floor of that car or that jeep and on the way to that place that smells. My *compañera* asks me why I carry a gun if I am a poet and if I am searched it will mean the end. You know why, don't you? We both know, and it was Rigoberto López Pérez helped teach us the value of arms here in the throat of the Americas. When I write, it is the words themselves, every one of the words, so unlike the *guardia* flies, that ask me whether... Well, I am not at all sure what it is that they ask. That is part of the struggle, and part of the presence I feel outside the door of this hut in the *barrio*. I am enclosing a pamphlet.

Leonel

Ombra Completa: A Translation from Sleep

Pardon me, but the surrealists are kept in a pen
back of the stadium. Join the line
that has been indicated. Please forgive me,
you will surrender up your papers here
and your pens there. Do as you are told.
You will now lift up your shirts
and undergo the examination for grief.
Do not be afraid. There is nothing much
to fear. I beg to differ with you,
put down your knapsack of words
here, right at my feet.
You will see I am wearing heavy boots—
there is nothing at all wrong in that.
In view of your size, you will be so kind as to
allow a brief moment of jocularity among the custodians.
There now—it is over and you only suffered,
did you not? Please feel free to ask questions
as you are expected to travel light.
I cannot answer for what goes on inside,
we have consultants from your own country
to assure you. There is a pile of rags
that you must now dive into. My goodness—
we are at home here, are we not?
You will please to hurry, for I understand
the stadium is becoming full.

You will hurry please now, the stadium is filling up.

The Freak Brothers

We were a crew like the Freak Brothers, living our lives out
in an American comic strip. The bomb was perfect,
well and truly armed,
in place at the rear of McDonald's
and in the middle of tea two miles away
we would slap our heads and remember—
the fucking safety was on, speed back
to the same building dropping briefcases
and losing whole walletsfull of stolen ID
to snap the one switch into place
that was the key,
without regard for the timer
reaching its appointed end—
one step around the corner and KABLLOOOOOEYYYY
everything flying at us,
witnesses staring and
us screaming across the street
with singed hair and jumping into the car
which now had a flat tire
pierced by a brick
and racing away
at a careful eye-catching hobble

singing, singing
at the top of our disguised voices
not "We Shall Overcome," but
"Let's Spend the Night Together."

It Works &

& it works when you least expect it & it works twice on birthdays & it works because you said yes to the brown acid & it works less as your hair grows & it works by making gardens into light years & it works where it wants & it works while you walk the dog & it works through others while you are sleeping & it works in French & it works on Pluto & it works sadly & it works through bodies you have known & it works & it works & it works &

The Little Bird

The little bird hides in drink
and in the machete used to lop off an arm

the bird sits right there on the stem
of your neck and whispers
that none of it is real
that none of it matters
that doing one thing is as good as
doing another
and doing nothing is just as good
as either

this damn bird
it sells itself to you
through fear
or through
your own grand desire
to become drunk
and listen to a song
you don't hear

he became drunk
he was pushed into a black International jeep
and pushed out again at the side of a road
with nobody on it
where three slugs were put into his
heart, his head and his balls
before his arm was
lopped off
and thrown away into the field

a totally random action
like the high note
in the little bird's song
as it sings
drunken
that nothing matters
that
it is all
the same

Mayakovsky

For Kim Terry Smith (1952–2003)

Mayakovsky,
when you kicked down the door to my brother's room,
you saw an army of ants on the march,
tanks rolling into the public square,
a yard of candlewick suspending a legal pound of plutonium,
a cranial saw undergoing a power surge,
several rabid bats,
& a fork impaling tainted meat.
Many of these things fled
& you picked my brother up out of his sad disposition,
you deposited your royalty cheques into his empty bank account,
you said to him he had hair worthy of the revolution,
a moustache worthy of any Mexican,
you said hello,
you said, here, smoke this,
and do not be upset forever,
& here, here is a ticket to the hospital,
to the Praesidium,
you have finally been nominated to the Senate,
there are those that trust you with their lives.

To put it simply,
is there anything that can be done?

What else matters? The sound from a speaker?
The hand in the hungry flywheel?
The globe?
The globe in chains?
A man kneeling?
Red?
Smoke?
A glacier and the shear of stone?
Shadows?

Perhaps the shadow of Mayakovsky outside the door of a room
by the oil tanks on Rideau street,
my brother locked inside?

Perhaps the shadow of Mayakovsky over my brother.

Goodbye, my family.   I enter a world in which you are
already holy. My brother in the sandbox, stemming
the flow of glacier
& blood streaming from my head.

South

It is good to have guests, of course,
and it is not good to have guests—
you never know when they will come for you.

You never know if when the rug is lifted
a squad of cockroaches will surround you,
a plague of ticks force you
into the heart of the sweating street,
into their secret places,
whether mice are tunnelling
so that your most secret sounds
will reach their quivering ears,
and you never know if the centipede,
Mister Centipede himself,
is marching past your small cone
of vision, you never know
about the ants and their levelling,
but what is more obvious
than the flies with TV camera eyes,
the mosquitoes sampling blood,
the dandruff that sleeps atop your head
only so it can hear your thoughts?

Even as they carry you off, you shout,
Why bother asking me anything?
You know it all.

That is the difference
between you.

Help Is Coming Cento

A fragment of the universe missing for centuries
All headed in more or less the same direction.

I'd hurl the creature to hell.
Who am I to give advice but I say yes—
Sometimes a leg is enough for a dog.

You are walking in a foot of water
A dilation, longing—
Ha, that was a night to remember!

And when the army's not available to carry us,
Stalin really should have shaved off that moustache.

Do what I say, no one gets hurt
In that bathroom that meant death.
Where will I put you, I wonder,
When they come for us rattling?

Ike Met Space Aliens

For Jubal Harshaw

1—Introduction

It'll be hard to train them suckers to appreciate golf
With three arms
The cure for cancer
And all of space to explore.

2—Mise-en-scène

Betty Crocker tugged Rin Tin Tin's leash.
Sorry, ma'am, but they were pretty specific—no dogs allowed.
Rin Tin Tin isn't a dog, soldier, he's an institution.
He looks pretty much like a dog to me, ma'am.
What race are you, boy?
I'm Eye-talian, ma'am, second-generation American.
Well listen here, my little Eye-talian, you don't let me through,
This American dog is going to bite your face off.
Rin Tin Tin does so.
Betty Crocker hurries across the tarmac, to where the space aliens are waiting for the president of the United States of America, the strongest nation in the world.
She mutters to herself, No immigrant is going to stop an American institution from seeing the space aliens.

3—Meanwhile

Power out. A bowl of warm milk on the steps of the White House. Two hot dogs with mustard and a coupla cokes. Sweet Marie chocolate bars. Keep watching the skies, and Jayne Mansfield's head brought up the back way in an ambulance. In the garage, two armoured limos and a ball of blue light.

"Cure her and you can have every Russian in the country." Ike is doing some hard dealing.

The space aliens are having none of it. They've brought their trade goods and a list of desired items. They're collecting sports figures this year.

Carl Jung is sucking oxygen from a tube in the corner.

Babe Ruth's palms sweat as he goes up to bat.

The gloves are coming off.

4—Flash to the Future

Ronald Reagan sits back and winks at the TV console. It burbles to life.

"Well, Ike, a fine mess now. You were a terrible horse-trader. Look at the evidence. We should have let them move on."

"I had no way of knowing, Ronnie. There was a decision to make." Ike's voice seems doubly disembodied today.

"Yup, pardner, let's tote up the benefits you got us—hydrogen fusion too early, Kennedy at all, Buckminster Fuller and airplane hijacking as subconscious sky worship. Nice. Hippies. Spaceship Earth. *Penthouse.* New wave music. The Black Panthers. Working from within the system as a viable alternative. The Pill. And now herpes. Damn it, Ike, they've given us herpes! I can't believe it!"

"Well, we don't know they did." A disembodied Republican on the defensive was something to hear.

"You *know* they did—they *look* like herpes, for God's sake!"

"You're being unfair, Ronnie."

"It's fine for you to sit back and be so generous. You're not out here in the front line. I've got the football and I don't know where the hell to run with it. Don't worry—I wouldn't ask you for advice. Never. I just wanted you to know that when I get over there there's going to be some behinds kicked and kicked hard. Believe you me, chrome dome."

"Commmmmmmmme onnnnnnnnn, Ronnnnnnnnie...."
Reagan wriggles his nose and cuts transmission. He's had enough grief for one day. He crawls down from the chair, crosses the floor of his office in about ten minutes of solid running and leaps into the ear tunnel at the side of the wizened head, nearly slipping on a puddle of pomade that had pooled on the floor at the base of the skull.

Ronald Reagan stands and, noticing a tiny drop of Brylcreem on the rug, wipes it with his toe. He idly fingers the itch in his left ear.

Back in the saddle again.

5—Beamed Down Commercially

... and uh say unto you that that there mugwump in the White House had better get down off his high and mighty and wear out his knees mighty quick because, my friends, my dear faithful, there is coming a day of judgment, and no little green thingies are going to be able to help him then, no sir, though they got stuff that might look mighty impressive to some. If you've read your Bible you know the Almighty God's got better weapons hid up his sleeve than somewhat that will flit around the sky like it's got its tail on fire.

Have faith, my friends, because there ain't no way the day will be long in coming—and though them thingies mighta brought Ike birth control and more coloureds, and though they mighta brought Raygun back to life, they ain't brought none of them the security nor the peace of mind we got in our tent here tonight.

Rise with me, sinners, and pray.

6—Down to It

Six Russian seamen snatched from ship in mid-Atlantic.
It is claimed to be an isolated incident.
"Six less commies," Ike exults on first hearing the news brief.
The top brass seem agitated.
The space aliens fidget all through the trade session.
G-man Hoover is the first to break. "Alright, you little wimps, confess! You don't scare me with any of your cutesie-pie gobbledegook—I'll give you back the sex ferret and Little Wang the cook and blow you to bits!"
"Herbie..." Ike is vegetable-like in his judgment but Hoover's panic reaches him slowly, like rays from a gun with no charge. They were testing that out in Los Alamos right now.
One little space alien's voice could be heard: "Low on tars and nicotine, smoked 'em ..."
WHAT? Half the table exploded. The tall thin green one they thought was the chief trader or at least the straight man stood and surveyed the table from chin level: "Never give our sucker a Russian mate...."
Consternation.
"Russians make the best tea ...."
"Take my ship ... please!"
In one corner of the room, the brass harangue Ike: "... digesting the *Communist Manifesto* ..." "... competitive volume of people to trade ..." "Can we stand the stress?"
The space aliens knew their schtick would help no longer. And it was too early to lay out their big demand in exchange for exclusive-rights offers. They had to punt. The space mitts were off.
In its musical whine, the one that looked the most like the Alka-Seltzer Boy explained: "We are right now training these seamen to be our assistants."
Pandemonium.
"We require one of our shows to be produced on your primitive television grid."

7—Cast

Phil Silvers was a space alien.
Mort Sahl was not.
Lenny Bruce was a space alien.
The Smothers Brothers were not.
On *The Dick Van Dyke Show,* Laura was a space alien but Rob Petrie was not.
On *I Love Lucy,* the Mertzes were. Everyone else was not.

8—Epilogue

You want words
I'll give you words—
scrEEEEEEEEE
jerksicle
mega-mega-mega-murdermeter
oMMMMMM neutralizer
pantworm—
these're all words
for things that really exist.
They were sold to the United States of America
by visiting space aliens
in nineteen-fifty-four.
You never hear of 'em?
No wonder—
they sold 'em in turn
to nazi-loving South American colonels
for torture.
Every one of 'em is in use
this second—
that's why there's so many flies up here
these days.
God—what burns me's they threw
the advisors in
for free.

On the Breaking of Discipline

Split lip
sucks wind.
This was your father.
A ghost came through the wall,
that was your mother.
Father kept death
wrapped in a baby blanket
in the hall closet.
Once a month
he aimed it
at the full moon.
You lived in the earthquake zone
of Southern Ontario.
You watched others grow
up straight
but you were in the heartland
of fear.
You knew better
than to remember.
You are hooked by blood
through lip
to seismic fluctuations.
You love the ghost
that makes a joke
of instability.
It knows the act of observation
alters that which is observed.

In the forest your father
leans over & aims his head
at a tree & fires.
The tree screams.

There is no one to hear.

The ghost is in you
dodging bullets
no one can see.

Forgot to Tell You

I heard you say it was French, I heard you say it didn't matter, that there was sand at the bottom no matter how far we fell, I heard them shout a warning, *hay peligro, tonto,* I heard one after another of my excuses burn away in the atmosphere, I heard you had died in the Toronto General without me.

Declarations of War

For Bess, a mutt, hit by a car on the Don Valley Parkway
the same moment I sat down to write

I'm sorry I never told my old black dog much of anything.

We walked for literal years, both on what we knew was the sharp end of the leash, while I chanted "arnie this, and arnie that" and real gems like "arnie and jim, jim and arnie."

I never told him why I stopped writing, or why I went to law school, or how I stopped drinking, or how I stopped smoking, or how I stopped breathing.

Never took him to Nicaragua, or back to my childhood, or up in my spaceship.

He was naked for sixteen years, then he died.

My favourite memory of Jo-Anne's memories of me is when she told me she'd seen me at 2 a.m. in the icy backyard picking him up and walking around, on legs that never worked again.

He kept whispering to me "jim and arnie, arnie and jim."

We bought him for thirty-seven dollars, which works out to just over two bucks a year, which is quite a bargain in the end.

Guerra Thrice

Twenty wars
Can't bring back Elmer the Safety Element
Can't untumour the american cloaca
You may as well stuff it with sandwiches.

The moon circled the earth urgently
Eyes played a stringy guitar
Crusted with red salt. Televised.
News watched by an indifferent dog.

Let's blot the copybook, let's
Send death to the war, let it think
It's off to see its mother.

I've been ordered to empathize
While my mouth is open, when there's
A horse in this room!

After "Guerra a la Guerra por la Guerra" by Rafael Alberti

13/4/83

Sure, and if I met one of my victims on the streetcar,
what the fuck do I do? Make conversation? Of course—
"That's a pretty interesting scar you've got there.
How do you use the phone with those fingers missing?
What the hell happened to your leg? Do you miss your
vision? Do you miss that or your hearing more?"
We ride together in silence,
me bending my eyes sideways to either assess the
damage or find the nearest excuse and hold it hostage.
It's the fucking residual guilt, man, of seeing what
you've done. Unlike the righteous indifference
of the CIA psychopath. Imperfect consciousness. A fuck
of a thing to suffer from. Especially when the victim
and I get off at the same stop and have to walk home
together. I feel like shit, but it makes me hate the
fucks at the top who make it necessary. Don't worry.
I see it. I do it. I just don't feel good after. Ever.

Then the victim begins abusing you. The victim
arrogates itself above you. Pull the safety back. Fire.

VIRUS

Virus A

Death dog runs down man in woods. A machine ticks away at the heart of ferocity. Hard-edged painting is like this. Ice melting is like this, but watching the rain drip like blood is nothing at all like it. It is its own corollary. There is a button to push. At dawn, death men enter woods to run down dog. His heart was missing. Tick machine tick.

Virus B

The animals that hide in briefcases, inside mufflers, in the car wash, under the mainframe. The animals are pulling on chains the size of a small artery, looking you in their eye, the artery, the small blind eye of the telephone, the wet stain of a mother in an operating room, the box camera of the reason, the reason itself like a false passport, several animals queueing up outside the last kiss, unfinished.

Virus C

The third night was always the most difficult.
Cries in the street and the text is full of errors.
The third night is the night of a full lunar eclipse, the night of fish swimming through alpha waves, of waiting for day like an appointment.
The night of reassurance that slow beginners cannot be faulted.
A night spent in petticoats, shorn by the tonsured darkness of creeping aphasia.
How far will it get tonight?

On the pier, God rents a helicopter for fifteen minutes.

Virus D

Penises fear the voice of women. As breasts fear the teeth of steroid babies. As woman's purse is a metaphor for the scrotum, a well-aimed kick is the cure for nothing at all. From one skin cell numerous bodies are cloned every night. If you turn on the lights quickly enough, the x and y chromosomes can be caught holding hands. Love is pure gristle and, in specimens shielded from religion, forms a ridge running along the spine to where a tail would be.

Virus E

You wake up one morning and you've never seen the colour blue.
No one told you.
You realize they all felt sad.
One hundred years of solitude sits on your bedside table.
Blake lies on the floor by your bed.
The Spicer book is beside the bottle of Canadian Club.
It is still life. With or without blue.
Your penis was bigger last night.
Technological terrorism.

Virus F

Blind eye swim fish blank right in the centre of the forehead. Search location radio pacing halls in sleep. A dead man died in this room. From igneous rock on water Steve sees shafting light upwards. He senses trouble in the grid. Robot ghost swims by slightly underwater. Cold literal drift. A man is erasing himself from his room. Outside a strip of birch bark crawls by on roof. Within the envelope fire and radio, to each other cold comfort. Erasure complete.

To Leonel Rugama in Nicaragua—Letter Two

Why do we bother writing to each other? So that a letter finally gets there and sits because the other has been murdered? Because in the composition we explain our ideas to ourselves? Because you will die, I will die, they will die, and it will or will not make a jot of difference in the world around us, and we want some record to be available someday that we were indeed on one side or the other? I have learned so very much from reading your booklet, that there is no difference between our struggles, in one sense, and that there is a world of difference in another. You have Sandino, we have Farabundo Martí. Virtually the same year, they died, were murdered. Our *matanza* stole how many lives—35,000? You have lost the same number in the course of more years.

Do we write then because we are the same person, grown up only several hundred miles apart, carrying out a doppelgänger life in which the same character gets to do different things but within a limited frame? As I close the doors and pull the shutters on my mother's house, lift the material from its place in the corner, and begin to tune the shortwave, do you speak nervously around the corners of your mother's house, and approach the corner where you unearth a poem?

Will my next letter tell you of a broadcast that I heard, or will one never arrive? Will your next enclose a poem or two, or blank sheets?

Why when I thought of you last night did I see myself?
Is the knock on the door innocent?
There are so many questions.
Others die. Because of our actions, independent of our actions, or, worse, in spite of our actions.
The living need us. As long as we do not forget the dead.

Con un abrazo fuerte

Roque

Message Remnant

Reader of lips!
Calculating
Bastard!
Extension
Of my self!

I've got your
Number—cough up
The heated core
Make silence
Explode
Or I'll put the
Finger on you
Once and for all!

The storm moves
Inside
The hairs
Of the inner ear
Stand erect

Discharge
Your responsibility
Avatar of tool!

Remove this
Distance!

Connect

Me!

I demand
...

Lachrymose

and when you come to me lachrymose demonstrating how the
bullet passed through your ugly little sheaf of poems,
each molecule of blood spilling from your wounds named
with the name of a hero or a martyr,
your smile full of teeth which, I am sorry, but it is
true, remind me of nothing more than the devastated
silhouette of Managua at dusk,
I see your books dog-eared in the Mercado Oriental, half
submerged in straw hats woven by weeping mothers,
I ask the young man in green fatigues and a face shining
from the sweat of having sat up all night on the curb
protecting his multiply-insufficient barrio from generic crime,
I demand of the Bank of America building proof of earthquakes
and the solidity of dangerous abstraction,
and your own brother who shucked the village then
the region then the very country of your birth
from his shoulders like, well, nothing so much as like a yoke,
I request the very air, the music, the fruits of the
earth of your too humble dress
a simple question
that deals with why and how and when and where and what
and, finally, deals with me

the answer is equally simple, I guess, I know, I am sure,
and they all answer, in unison of course,
¡presente!
which, translated, means he is here, means he never left,
means he will always be with us, and so on, you get the drift,
we will never forget you, and all those things
that are said and unsaid and cried out and whispered,
and I find myself
speaking to you
here

I Am Amazed

Wake up.

I dreamt K-Mart
Into existence!

The same day
I dream K-Mart,
I will be there
In the store!

How many men
Realize
Their dream
So
Quickly?

The road is tortuous!
The future is bright!

Open the doors!

This Just In

Tanks have surrounded the Parliament Buildings in Ottawa, the Prime Minister's residence is under siege by heavily armed men in civilian clothes, Cardinal Carter has been shot in the face and the heart while delivering the Easter homily and is presumed dead, there are currently thirteen mayors being held hostage, the border community of Prescott has been attacked, oil storage tanks in Kingston have been blown up, three Oshawa union leaders have been found with signs of torture, there are several unidentified body parts in the local waste-disposal site, the offices of the *Toronto Star* were firebombed again today for the third consecutive day, no one has seen the head of the CBC for weeks and speculation is rife, the group entered the town of Belleville from the north shortly before midnight and gathered together the women and children and men separately, shot randomly into the crowds and raped a number of women before performing atrocities upon their bodies, the military has ordered University of Toronto and York University closed indefinitely with no explanation, the OPP travelled from Wawa to Moosonee rounding up young men and pressing them into service, hunting down those who have fled, crops are burning near Chatham, sporadic small arms fire is heard as this is typed, it is a normal day, it is an election day, U.S. media reports that an overwhelming number of us have expressed our confidence in the system.

After Vallejo's This/Happened Between Two

If you succeed in palpitating, then tremble
In the vein, get sick, drink to excess,
Drink enough to achieve equilibrium,
To start the fire that will placate me.

Remain an alcoholic, it's your decision,
But look out for the major, the sober one from the army,
Without teeth, but believe me, a frightening one.
He'll make you swim in bad water.

May you then remain alcoholic,
A grand notion, and jump up into the sky.

What a useless arpeggio, this death
Coming to you: drink up the red
Among five sub-lieutenants
Who admire you, who really admire the abyss.

Decide that a hint is enough,
maybe even just to touch it:
decide there is no death except in acquisition—
sure, go for religion all of a sudden, tomorrow
stick his shoe in your damn mouth.

Understand death, colonel
Of death, he's in charge of the camp,
Has me in proxy misery, I'm really a sad one,
For the night of us all.

Never let him get you alone
And revise your schedule—
His henchmen broke my vertebrae, my tongue!

Coda

who is this small man
who gathers round him evidence
of absurd hope
he is the New Guinea man bowed low
before a Sony radio
he is Wovoka the shaman
travelling for the first time
between tribes
sure in his faith
the ghost dance will banish
all evil
he is I–and–I who stand on the shore
as the sun rises on one big ship
black as the sun
eclipsed
he is a small man
in the face of the lion
in the face of the CIA virus
in the face of the eclipse

his heart
its rich red warm beam
cuts the dark
despair

One Hundred Most Frightening Things

A

Finding, waking, phone off hook
A man forcing her, getting rough
Rosedale ravine leapover impulse
Her crying mouth trembling unsure line
Blood in the toilet, paper red
Her loss of face
Men with suntans all over their bodies
Loss of all her papers I keep—yes
The loss of any sum of money at all
I never want to see you again

B

Touching shit with my fingers
The droplets I see fly from coughing people
Post-coital disease admissions
Lumps
The sight of doctors and nurses in social situations
Sucking wounds
Large organs of any kind exposed
Surgery documentaries
Deep holes in ground
Shortage of breath

C

I'm sorry that's the wrong answer
What do you mean
I never want to see you again

I'm attracted to you
What did you do all night
What are these stains
Why didn't you just phone me
Where is the money you owe us
Died died died died died
Let's go to bed

D

Police
Store clerks
Priests and ministers
Athletes
Published writers as a descriptive term
Corporation executives who are not ugly
Doctors nurses ambulance drivers nurses' aides RNAs
  dieticians psychiatrists lay counsellors dentists
  and associated receptionists
Musicians who have slept with more than one woman
The intrusion of brothers and sisters
Women women women jesus god women

E

Christopher Dewdney's poems
Jean Genet's novels particularly *The Thief's Journal*
Wayne Clifford's seeming content with not writing a word in years
David McFadden's inane crazy wisdom via southern Ontario
  meaninglessness
Jack Spicer dead César Vallejo dead Picasso dead Man
  Ray dead Duchamp dead Tzara dead Pound dead Dewdney
  dead Genet dead Clifford dead McFadden dead
Robert Heinlein writing about politics

Jennifer Clark never publishing
The decomposition of paper
The distinct possibility of triviality
Offending my mother offending my mother

F

Single hairs growing in inappropriate places
The statistically improbable
The virtually certain
The unavoidable solution
The vomit of small domestic animals
The necessity of pronouncing words I have never heard spoken
Chance encounters with cancelled acquaintances that necessitate
  reminiscence about events I do not remember
Arranged meetings with strangers who are taller than me
Being caught masturbating by cleaning staff or lovers
  who come home at unexpected times
Fire

G

The imprisonment of Ulrike Meinhof
The jungle despair of Che Guevara
The seedy hotel defiance of Milton Acorn
The impossibility of supporting my mother
The stupidity of the masses dressed up as anything else
Rhetoric
The distinct possibility of writing meaning nothing other
  than a mode of temporal dislocation
Rhyming couplets written by living women
The moment before I know whether she will undress
Determination of friends

H

Alcohol
Acid
Cocaine
MDA
Testosterone
Adrenaline
Women who talk casually of the eating of the afterbirth
Perfume made from animal parts
Sodium nitrate
Blood outside natural boundaries

I

Stars that change position suddenly
Words that when reread change their meaning
Ambiguous utterances of lovers
Muttered ejaculations of nighttime drivers
Incompletely heard warnings
Thoroughly justified and verifiable citations of personal irresponsibility
Innocuous statements of friends who are mentally unstable
Prayers
Bulk mailings
Silence from a woman in bed

J

Once upon a time
If only
Despite the fact that
Never again
Only if
Surely you could have
Why didn't you
That's okay for you to say
Maybe sometime
Next time

A Species a Second

for Laura Mackew

Pogo was found nailed to a tree in Okeefenokee
Daisy was backed over by Herb on a bender
Heckle & Jeckle succumbed to avian flu
Chip went off his meds & filleted Dale.

Huey & Dewey warned Louie not to come one day
& took out 17 goslings at the hatchery,
One poisoned weiner in the park
Took Rin Tin Tin out real good.

Garfield lost one then two legs to diabetes
Snoopy drank until his liver burst
Tweety got swallowed &
Sylvester died of the blockage.

It is so lonely, it is
So lonely.

Heycoo

A white poodle was bitten
By yellow teeth in a container.

This old bus turns three corners.

The Toll

I dream I've left
The phone unhooked
Upstairs in the lab.
The ocean is pouring in,
Starfish drift
Through a rift in my head.

Soft-lipped fish
Gather round my nipples.

My hands, my back
Drenched.

At last, at last
Swept away!

Drink lovingly at dawn
From the well again,
Wash sweat
From my clammy brow,
Scales and muddy
Footprints from the floor.

Melly, Edward, Robert
Drowned in their beds.

Investigative Loss

How it was lost,
how it got taken away,
how it was absorbed.

How it disappeared in the night,
how it was erased from the tape, just
how the signal was scrambled,
how the image was lost,
how it faded away.

How it got carried off,
how it was arrested and jailed,
how it fell into a hole in the earth,
how it was here no more,
how it got hidden,
how it evaporated,
how it melted away.

How mine wasn't there,
how yours was misplaced,
how it slipped her mind,
how no one knows where it is,
how there is no map,
how no message was left,
how there is no address,
how there is no number,
how thin air swallowed it up,
how it might be among papers,
how it was just here one minute ago.

How it is covered up,
how someone might have taken it away,
how it came to be other than where it was.

How there is a sense of loss.

After Vallejo's Well Does the Pallid Metalloid Heal You?

Well? Your health is a pale, pale metal.
The metal burns, civilian.
To which holiday spot do you want your ashes sent?

Exclaim, and travel in circles.
A lethal dose forms at your portal,
Your guttural asshole, all the corridors, the arteries.

Mister Exclamation, tomorrow is magical,
See for yourself, finally,
The bust of your tremulous placidity,
Suffer, throw yourself on the mercy of the shoemaker,
Pass your last good organ, out of three separate assholes,
Laugh, fluid by fluid,
Down to the senator's claim on your birthcord,
You blood llama,
Living below the house of the dead,
Feel inclined to have fought a little harder,
See—one moment, they tell you when it's past.

A gallon of some things is infinitely enough, for each:
The dirty earth resulted from their hunger for dirt,
You retreated from the junta to the hermitage,
Turning one obscure colour after another,
Never looking back to correct your connection to the womb.

See that man over there, the one who speaks so well?

Do the metals give you a little pain in advance?

Don't Forget Alberti

Hey—hey, yeah, you!
Right down here.
In this dirty old box.
I'm Rafael Alberti's poems &
I can't fucking get out!

Let me out—hey, *cabrón,*
Don't walk away from me,
This is Rafael Alberti's *obra*
Strangling in a cardboard box
Outside the back door
By the stairs down to the plaza, *sí,*
Right here in the hot sun
In Frigiliana.

I can open up new worlds.
I can cure that limp, sister.
I'll whisper to you
Who took the Lindbergh fucking baby.

I went away,
I stayed away,
I came back when that porcine
Mound of maggot shit finally
Started rotting.

This is the thanks I get?

Do not walk away.
Do not walk away from me.
Do not walk that way.

One Thousand Nine Hundred Thirty Words

One thousand nine hundred thirty words
Burning like the earth
From inside out
But there is no smell—they make no stink
They make no smoke
And when they are gone
There's a word for that.

I'm not telling you anything you don't know
I was just a curious passerby
An alphabet in the making
A registry of fetches and hexes
A real eating pissing pooping machine
With sound effects.

I woke up that first morning
Wrapped up in a body.
It got weirder, school hurt
People hurt, and words comed out
Hanging round in little bunches
That would try and separate themselves
Offer discounts
Take holidays.

I invented science as much as anybody
I looked through broken glass at a sky
Only I saw, full of pop and chips
And chocolate bars and acid, saw missiles
no one spoke about.

I peered at the International Brigades
From a stepladder propped against Everest.
Of course it slipped and I fell for years,
Desperate as hell, abysswards
With only a cup of milk to tide me over.

Not everything was about me
I was just a museum
A book open to the page before the colophon
Where the credits are stored.
Someone won, so I walked, my vocation
Unable to wean the sin from the saint
Trembling at the very gate
Where the electrical storm stands guard.
I just couldn't figure it out
This says what I saw, *nada más*.

I never saw Gandhi fight the salt laws
I never saw the pope convulsed with laughter
Over the fate of the soviet union, some
Idiot prince flying back to Poland.

This doesn't mean that I can escape blame
For anything, it's not like I'm a
Croat shot in a crowded execution
Who had to go suddenly
Who got tranquil the day
Portugal was freed.

The trick is being born in a year when
You can escape being enslaved, exterminated, incinerated
Or hit by a meteorite, a year when
Assassins are tranquil, when astrologists
Work in a factory, a year when
I had a mother.

I'm so mad now I could rain, my feet burst from my shoes
And mumble, brothers would have been good
It would have been nice to have a brother.

After "1930," by Nicanor Parra

The Cuban Missile Crisis

At the first sign of trouble, Lassie barked up a 12-foot extension ladder, Rin Tin Tin leapt & crow-boys Heckle & Jeckle raptured him to guard position on the landing struts of Sky King's Cessna.

The gang patrolled the skies & scared off all communists, & landed back at the ranch in time for Penny's birthday cake.

Hence there was no crisis, but for the short bald homeless man raving at the bushes in Gorky Park that he would bury them all, slammed his one hand-held shoe to an invisible table, laid down his head on his peasant's arms, & wept.

Me, I never looked up, I was cramming for quiz shows by reading all the Classics Illustrated comic books at once.

Tiny aliens danced along the barrel of my gun.

The Corpse

I stood and watched one more word crawl out of his mouth, and I had to turn away. The head rested in a vast puddle of words, the smell was loud, and the body still heaved and twisted with the words struggling to escape. By the time I turned to look again, the corpse was smothered in them, small colonies moving off in tiny bursts of sound.

No Pasarán

Franco ate beans for lunch.
But he wanted to eat Madrid.

The brigade was mixed salad
Congealed on the edge of an old plate.

So many smelly militiamen
Floating down the river Ebro!
Shoot me! Shoot me! Shoot me!

There are hounds in the Ebro, Madrid!
There are flags in the trash can!
I'm the only bridge left standing
From here to Republica!

To Nibbles, My Dog

To Nibbles, my dog-child
Who knew nothing at all, your eyes said
As much as tobacco, dumb enough, your glance.
But you had big shoulders to get up over things
And when you left me, you had no spine.
Look at other dogs, all worked up, orphanistic, save them!
But you just improvised, rotting old Nibbles
As you whirled around in your scared fits
Which brought my house down in fear.
Despite all the drives to the ambulance, we didn't
Because it was filled up with the naked dead
And you had bitten the child in me
While we wrestled up in the air, landing on some poor prostitute.
But you were my best friend.
Your dog family didn't get it
They didn't want to get it
And the number of times you sold me,
Nibbles, comrade!
You made a mystery of me
The way I ran into the street that day.
Sure you were happy, sure you were happy,
Happy dog.

After "A Niebla, mi perro" by Rafael Alberti

After Parra's Self-Portrait

Consider, *muchachos,*
Being in conversation with the frail beggar.

Or, say, a professor with an obscure licence,
He, the one who lost the voice of the *hacienda* class.

Dispute from death to taxes
The hag's scarred but seminal horse.

Which of us appears dearest when demented?

Truly, that inspires lasting self-arms escalation!

Who decides to zap the blacks,
What intervention of art is there in that part-sin?

Why I Am Such a Nice Guy

I ran away from a fight at sixteen.
When the detectives came for my brother I was relieved it wasn't
  for me.
I wished my father dead.
I make my own best excuses.
I only read a few books.
I was glad when my ex-wife had children with another man.
Last year I smashed a glass into my palm when angry.
This year was much better—I broke my knuckle hitting a door in anger.
I slapped an alcoholic in the head two years ago.
I pray people don't die, then worry it is because I don't want to be
  inconvenienced.
I came home at 3 a.m. to find her drinking the going-away champagne,
my laundry clean and folded at her feet.
There have been times I have wanted sex at any cost.
I broke my sister's collarbone when I was six.
I cut my brother's head open with a plate when I was eight.
Because I am angry and cannot express it.
I feel distant love for my brothers and sisters.
I feel left out.
I spent a whole summer neglecting her for another woman who wanted
  none of me.
I feel lust for the fourteen-year-old in the kitchen.
I doubt myself.
I don't read enough.
I feel an unholy thrill when people I admire like me.
I tremble before job interviews.
I have skipped job interviews and lied about them.
I feel more warm and loving at a distance.
I fantasize best about expressing it at a distance.
I am even using this writing to get you to like me.
I eat out of the pot when I am alone.
I feel physically dirty.
I admire content rather than form.

I write only when I feel like it.
I am orally fixated.
I cannot remember my dreams.
My psychiatrist is in England.
It hurt me and cost me a lot to type that.
I am fussy about my own living space.
I am too obedient.
I am not trustworthy.
I am irresponsible in the extreme.
I am only confessing this so you think I am a nice guy.
I talk about friends behind their backs.
I want you to be my friend.
I talk too much.
I could go on forever.

The Morning Before High Noon

For Gene Day

They prophecied that ink would run today. Alley Oop pulled up in a borrowed Batmobile. Sluggo his muscle & that slut Nancy to play China Doll. Because Captain Canada is holed up in the Haunted House & his contract's at an end. The Syndicate is ditching him. He sensed it early. He's called in his friends, but they're stuck in the mail & he knows he's doing it alone. He's afraid, but he's been up against the toughest & he's still there.

Oop is not missing a trick—he piles newsprint all around, he'll burn the sucker out & beat him to death. The early morning Dagwoods & Blondies gather, sensing the wrong. Mary Worth at home with a broken hip & Doc Morgan out of town.

The sun rises the morning before High Noon & papers fetch up on concrete steps. There is nothing but smoke in the Haunted House. Grey matter rising in the wind. Night bleeds into the frame of day.

At 5 a.m. they find Gene Day, popular local cartoonist, face down in the street.

Lives of the Poets

I

John Wieners

John Wieners was found dead
In space, he withdrew
His face from circulation,
He had lived a fiction, bottling
Words, until the bottle contained nothing.
The setting was tears, the country
Was us, the discipline
Was drink. No he never returned
But his power passed
The bottle, in which words trapped
Poured cold collapse
Into Spicer, who lay
In a suppressed bed, debilitated, so many forms
He twisted himself into the bottle
Coming & going, rhyming reason
Inversely, one of his last words,
Broke wind for a duration
& Blaser grieved for complicated academics
Writing complicated poems, translations
You'd run from on the street.

Here, hold this,
While I carry Milton Acorn home,
Will you?

II

Jones

Daniel Jones I never seemed
To give a shit about you when you lived
So you are the perfect suicide
To take my confession.
I have no right to use your name,
Did not even know your address.
Christ, we all walked around on stilts
That made us much smaller, some
One said I felt so small
It took a whole country to fill me up.
Mr. Nicaragua, I had a full-body
Sandinista tattoo.
Daniel Jones, you were some
communard golem
who wrote, walked naked,
tried to outrage & left.

III

bpNichol & my dog arn

Poorest of the poor
Meekest of the meek
Arnest of the arns
Beepest of the beep

Arnie & beep went for a walk
Arn thought he walked beep
& beep knew who walked who

Beep sang to arn
& arn joined in
They sang about my brother Kim

Who died
Poorest of the poor
& meekest of the meek

They sang
Kim was thin
He had a brother Jim
Whom he had never seen

Yet there were pictures
Them together, 6 and 5
But the pictures are lost
& no witnesses survived

So there are no pictures
So they never existed
They died,
Meekest & poorest
Beepest & arnest

The body sucks
So much

You Envy Me

You likely know all this.
I was awarded the Prix Goncourt for how my legs grew pale and wasted.
They gave me the Victoria Cross because I had never had children.
The Pat Lowther Award came almost too easily, for the supper I promised but did not cook for Jo-Anne on May 10, 2008. We had pizza instead.
The Genie was a surprise, for how I once stood indecisively on a sidewalk for over two hours.
I feel I earned the Governor General's Prize for my lifetime of listening to the radio.
My failure to learn a single verb conjugation in twenty years got me the Gabriella Mistral medal two years in a row.
I was particularly humbled by the call about the Nobel Prize, based it seems on my inability to ask Mark Strand a single intelligent question in an interview in 1981.
My initial discomfort at the proposal to award me a full decade of the Noranda Prize for journalism about mines and mining was dispelled by the promise of confidentiality.

It's not like I seek these things out.
I would be just as happy toiling away in a refrigerator factory
or candling eggs on a factory farm owned by GayLea Foods.

I crave anonymity.
I crave more space in the backyard to bury these things, yet
even that, even that has brought me a beautiful wall certificate from neighbourhood dogs.

So please hear me out.
I declare, as of this moment,
a complete moratorium.
I will accept no further honours.
I will return all your congratulatory emails.

I ask that you honour my wishes in this.
I know for a fact you will read this
and I know you will want to fire off a letter to everyone you know
about how my recognition must not be delayed another second.
Don't.

Please.

Take up roofing instead.

Song of the Caller

Lead me out
Of this desert
To the river
Of dreams
Pouring out
Of my forehead

Hand above the flood
Floating by you
There is no crest
But your attention

Without you there
Is nothing tangible

I am swallowing time
By the mouthful

Ledger Entry

Tonight it takes my mother 48% of her income
To pretend she has a hold on this cubic space.
Tonight it takes all the money my brother will ever get
To line up the beer bottles his ghost will come back through.
Tonight they are tearing down low-rental houses here in my heart—

This is called planning for the future.

Tomorrow's hand trembles as it collects the rent
Aware of the stink on its fingers—
It is the offalous past offending the future,
If the future smells such things.

But tonight the rum ignores the improper use of electrodes
Throughout this hemisphere—
The peacefulness of night on the forgetful moon
Plays games with my human rituals—

Tonight is rent night:

My mother gave fifteen more days away.

War Review

Others may feel differently. I can't really rate World War II, but I think it smelled like pumpkin. Korea was like running a finger over sandpaper someone had spit on. The Suez War was like a sweet hot banana *à l'épicerie,* but segued almost entirely into the ball-grating citric elephant that was the Indochina War. It sat on a back shelf, spoiled, and was remarketed as *bombe aux Vietnam.* Then the world fell like a string of putrid aspic dominoes. War since has been as bland as day-old blood, taste of flour and snot, charred by fieldmice for a palate as flat as ebola.

Prayer

Oh great teddybear of the left, cushy
inside worker at the heart
of the party organ,
come out, come out, today is Monday,
we start at the foot
of the workweek
and climb.

It is time for a new order,
time to jump-start the revolution,
hotwire the imagination
of the baobabs and heffalumps,
the bambis whose delicate ears
are precious too to the cause.

The weekend of surveillance is over—
Mordor's microphones cough out smoke & fumes,
the metallic eyes of the dark lord wobble
on their stalks. They could not believe
their mechanistic senses, what they saw
was clearly impossible.
Ming's troops have all called in sick.

So let us begin again by giving up
our taste for socialist art,
let us start afresh
by dressing up in coloured clothes
& vie with each other
for the funniest praxis.

The prisoners will not disappear
& the tortured will still have to be tortured

for a while,
but they will hear us out here
& know we have not forgotten ourselves,

know we are coming for them,
making a joyous noise.

Barcelona Dream

For Blake

Let's walk down Las Ramblas till Nixon comes back from the dead,
till they drive a wooden stake through the heart of Washington,
till Pound seizes the portfolio, till we have enough to buy a potato
in a new world clean'd of hate.

TELEGRAMS

1

EX-LOVER DON'T COME BACK STOP CATS DEAD APARTMENT BURNT
STOP FRIENDS INFORMED OF YOUR TREACHERY STOP
I DIDN'T INTEND IT THIS WAY DASH BUT YOU GOT ME MAD

2

MAN BURIED IN GRAVE STOP PLASTIC TUBE TO SURFACE STOP
LAST SANDWICH EATEN STOP HANDS TIED STOP WATER GONE STOP
KIDNAPPER DEAD BY CAR STOP HALFWAY TO PHONE BOOTH

3

HAVE JUST SEDUCED YOUR NEW LOVER STOP
SO THERE STOP
HA

4

SAW YOU GO THROUGH POCKETS IN MY DREAM STOP
THE ADDRESS WAS A FAKE

5

PLEASE FORGIVE ME STOP I ONLY DID IT ONCE STOP
I DIDN'T ENJOY IT

6

Epilogue

CHILDREN OF THE FUTURE AGE STOP READING THIS INDIGNANT PAGE
STOP KNOW THAT IN A FORMER TIME STOP LOVE STOP
LOVE EXCLAMATION MARK WAS THOUGHT A CRIME STOP
THEY'VE CAUGHT THE ONE-ARMED MAN

Campo de Batalla

For Tellez

I

Eugenio has a gun pointed at his right temple.
There is no one else in the room in which
Eugenio has a gun pointed at his right temple.

This is no Saigon street execution, this is not a Nazi trooper
mailing in a standard *coup de grâce,* this is not the cow
he saw fall into the sea whom the sailors shot.

The gunman in this photo is as close to Eugenio
as someone can get to Eugenio, better placed
yet unable to talk that gun down.

It is a gross tool
for so fine a pain. I close the catalogue,
one sound muffled.

A little painted shell casing
plinks at my feet.
I hope he shot at me.

II

Have you heard this one?
Two skeletons cross a field marked as a map,
one armed one not.

When I first came to Europe I adopted
a different identity, I never took off
the night vision goggles.

My dog Firpo ate visitors.
My students loved me for all the wrong reasons.
I made sure my canvasses were taller and wider than me.

At 70 I remain curator of my youth.
I climb a ladder back to Chile
alone.

Street Survival

I

Street Survival is for all of you—
unless you are alert,
aware and disciplined,
your chances of surviving are poor.

You need to acquire the ability and equipment
to protect yourself.
You need the skills and tools
that will give you control.

This requires that you gain
the know-how to function independently
of whatever systems might break down.

Crime and violence are everywhere—
systems so complex that a simple malfunction
can have a domino effect
on others.

The most important factor
in the survival equation
is you.

Street Survival is for all of you.

II

Just below the strata of possession is found the layer of thieves. Breaking glass at midnight. Compression has caused these two layers to interpenetrate in exact equivalence to the symbiosis that actually arose.

Running feet.

Just below the strata of certainty, almost a veneer on the antithetical underlay, almost always on the verge of shatter.

Just below the strata of sex is found an image of the human figure undergoing distortion. Yes—that's it. Right there. Bend over and examine it precisely. The cleft of flesh has been reduced to rock-like node that must be passed through a hole too small for it. Observe the wave-like afterimage.

Just below the threshold. There it is—another threshold. Too trite to be subject to belief. That is it about the layer mode of observation—it goes on and on.

Time to go.

III

Weapons You Never Thought Of

"When you lack in strength and size, pick up something to equalize."

These are bludgeons. You should learn from history. Mimic the actions of an opposition party when in the company of well-heeled radicals. Assume the stance of the righteous when you find yourself in the pre-power stage.

These are different bludgeons. Take the chair you sit in and smash it over the skull of the first person who enters the room. Declare this person, if this works, an enemy.

Steal two children. Bring a woman. Board a small boat full of state-of-the-art electronic equipment. Take the boat to a position designated by the firm you work for off the coast of an enemy in South America. Allow just enough leakage to draw military craft. Assume persona and call for help to civilian station in the most ingenuous part of your country. Contact the nearest reactionary media. Induce a diabetic attack of massive proportions in the crippled child you have stored for the purpose. Politicize. Draw full pension.

Realistically, to be effective and used to its full potential, an improvised weapon must be handled with a certain degree of skill.

During the argument, throw it in his face.

When she turns her back, kick as if you were kicking a football. Aim for where her cock would be.

When you are finished with the manacled young man, use the two-by-four to stop breathing function, turn him off, and mix lime with the earth.

Look at me—I am thirty-one years old, five foot seven, one hundred and sixty pounds of sweetness and light. My Bauer running shoe can kill you in six ways. My black combat fatigue pants are a garotte, a stinging eyepoke, a gag of immense and deadly proportions depending on depth of penetration. My light brown t-shirt says "look out—I'm dangerous" in the most disarming of scripts. Beware—I am sentient, and thus fully armed.

My hands are registered as dangerous weapons, the old man said.

IV

The Extreme Reach Advantage of the Belt

In a real confrontation you would attempt
to strike for the knife hand.

An improvised stabbing weapon
seldom has a sharp cutting edge.

Use your tongue.

The most effective improvised weapons
in the home are found.

If you manage to penetrate the body,
don't pull it out immediately.

The best improvised weapon
is your awareness
coupled with your imagination.

Use your imagination.

Bunt me with your head.

That's not the impact of a bullet:
that's the idea of the impact
of a bullet.

The Finger

j'accuse
j'accuse the drunk men in overcoats and sweaters
in the middle of May on Parliament Street
they are grey
I accuse them of carrying all they own close to their skin
j'accuse the girl of Shoppers Drug Mart
whose nipple stayed out of sight
j'accuse the black felt pen hatred on the back
of the streetcar seat
j'accuse the beer I had for lunch
the bile that ran into my stomach
like blood
the anger
the anger

I accuse the memory of your mouth on the dead
forehead of my cock
j'accuse the blue plaid shirt I forgot in North Sydney
in another life
and the socks, the socks
whose price goes up
forever
and the memory of masturbating into one
and the girl behind the bedroom wall I have never seen
whose orgasms are a nightly fixation
and the ugly ugly sound of a man grunting like a pig
Circe, Circe
you too have wounded me
this is hardly sufficient to explain
j'accuse BIC ballpoint pen medium 29 cents
of being a servant of the realm
and the lack of a man in my mother's life
the fact that tomorrow is finite and yet incalculable
and that I might die before doing anything

j'accuse Philip Mason, that yankee bastard, of trespass
in my backyard when I was angry with him
and the table I write on for its individuating creak
myself of beating the cats
and the cats of being beaten too easily
the unworthy men who have made love to the women
I have known
the paper I write on of being white
only superficially
the men and women who follow me around
a little ahead of me and get the good jobs
and the people I have worked with
of taking me for granted
the people I have worshipped
of taking me for granted

j'accuse easy laughter
and the nun in grade five who told me
never to sing
j'accuse the habit of just
mouthing the words
and of silence
obedient silence
resentful silence

j'accuse the cigarettes
j'accuse the alcohol
j'accuse the cholesterol
and the carbohydrate
the protein
and the tears
of just going through me to get
somewhere

j'accuse health
and I accuse sickness

I accuse Nietzsche of hiding the answer
Selwyn Dewdney of not having me for a son
Wayne Clifford of not having me as a brother
Hugh Smith for having me as a son
j'accuse the shortness of my favourite jeans
and the cyst on my forehead
of both being sent from heaven

the door of the Don Jail
M.C. Escher, Titian
Piranesi
and the Kingston Psychiatric Facility
I accuse the opening line of *Howl*
of excellence and insufficient truth
j'accuse channels 17 and 19 the educational channels
of never being strong enough to win the wrestling match
with Tom and Jerry, Huckleberry Hound or *Fireball XL-5*
j'accuse Brian Inkster of gypping me
of several comic books
a week for the whole year I was 8
j'accuse the age of 8 itself
and 17
and 29
j'accuse the draft
and the dream of knights charging into a bathtub
in a long stream of teenage guilt

Robin Hood of lying to me about the world
and the Canadian Shield
and the concept of protection

the notion of predilection
and diversion

j'accuse the ones huddled within four walls
which are a prison they are not worthy to escape
and the ones who never stay home
j'accuse the sentences,
phrases, phonetic units,
the *cédilla*, the *umlaut*, the *accent grave*
all these I accuse

the sulky ones
the bold ones
the ones who never call
the ones who see clearly the most pallid side of satisfaction

I accuse myself, as I do the comma
that dot which feels itself wagging its own tail
as it disappears

I accuse you Kingston
who always waited outside
who did not love me
all who did not love me

j'accuse the Shroud of Turin of being insufficient cause
for revolution
the notions of zen buddhism and *Soldier of Fortune*
equally

the boojum
the snark
the epiphenomenon

and the structuralist rooming house
in Cabbagetown

someone must blame these holes in my wall,
someone must blame everyone awake at this moment,
as they must blame the sleeping
j'accuse the hair growing inside my lungs
delicious soft fur of death

and I abjure the noise my heart makes
in your silent night

I accuse the lack of tune in my living.

John

In that dream, I fought John Wayne. It started with our fists and I was amazed by the look of surprise on his face just before his sledgehammer blow knocked me out. When I stood, the six-gun was hot in my hand, and as I raised it I heard a strange barking sound coming from his hand, bandaged as it was. Taking one in the shoulder, I fell and picked up the M-16 that lay there at hand. Firing from a prone position, I was able to see the pin he pulled from the thing he threw as I thought I'd winged him, and after the smoke had cleared I could see him sitting at a console that mirrored the one where I sat, panting. Partway to the red button, both of our fingers halted, and he turned to me, and said well sonny I think I might just join you. I stood and walked toward him, wary and scared as hell. His handshake hurt as much as the first punch in the face he had given me as a child.

Playing Golf with the Colonels

Somoza cheats. When Duarte and I aren't looking,
he wedges several human teeth into the green.
This allows a roll to the right
and an extra stroke—Somoza wants to prolong
the game. Duarte claims first shot
at the caddy. I have to convince them
not to lead an assault directly on
hole eighteen from hole three—they are impatient
for total domination of the field.
Each spectator wears sunglasses, fatigues,
and a throat mike. We chat about the stockholders
and discover that we all attended the same high school.
It was full of unusually cruel boys who dragged
us all into the washroom and tried to cut
our hair. We all had vowed never
to be in that position again.
Somoza cannot see the ball clearly. An aide leaps
from the gallery, detonates a land mine,
and a few seconds later it is a clear shot.
Duarte turns to me and complains, stating
he would have just hired someone to carry the ball
into sight and then disposed of him.
He is a subtler man. He has earned
a reputation for seeking innocence
through the admission of guilt.
I begin to worry, because it is he who had promised
to pay for lunch.

The Schwarzenegger Poems

For compañera Nora Astorga

WHAT IS IN THE HEART OF AMERICA

a big kid
afloat on popcorn and pop
in a carnival his dad owns
looking for heroes

THE IMPORTANCE OF BEING ARNOLD

I

public transformation
nothing to hide
from the smilish Ivanhoe of *Pumping Iron*
through the sword extension
of multiple Conans
fully blossoming
like a stocky flower
over which a lawnmower
has recently run
in the various arcana
of ex-major and ex-colonel
eternally called back to active service
against your will
or by the trickery of friends

2

this moment
is the moment of your ripeness
now
an unacknowledged legislator
of a better morality
than seen stateside
since McCarthy
I mean this sincerely
I am not dissembling
nor mocking
you are not dogmatically anti-communist
you are not an assassin, as you have said
more than once
you are the consummate
rescuer

the seeker
after a peace of rest
from which you rail
at being woken

3

perhaps it is because you
are a democrat
transplanted from the fecund soil
of Europe

wronged
you wish only to right
and rest

tricked
you will sometime forego revenge
as revenge

4

you are not without fault
I wish to make my objectivity clear

you relate best to men
in particular, father figures, ex-employers
(if benevolent)
and men who resemble yourself
from your last mission together
in a flexible past

your body has become planar
losing the perfect roundnesses
of Mr. Universe
to the urban ideal
of perfectly functional icon:
the box, or container
sculpted, detailed, but innately insistent
upon rising

you are, in deed as in word,
the perfect phallus
a beacon
for your audience

5

none of which is satiric
I find wholly admirable
your tendency to make of dialogue
haiku

you are witty, trenchant
and tersely glib
what more can I say

you have caused more than one
to hang on a word

some you drop:

"I let him go."

others you instruct:

"Let's party."

The implacable, you merely observe:

"If it bleeds, we can kill it."

I imagine you
far more intelligent
than most actors

MY OPENING ARGUMENT

Sure, it's a fantasy; just because the last ten years
has given a terrible smell to hero worship,
like any drug,
in moderation it's good for you.
This man is convincing.
He knows his own limits
and when he has no limits
and is not afraid
to speak tongue-in-cheek
deadpan.
He is widely misunderstood.
He is lumped in with Stallone, Norris and Bronson.
He has many imitators.
He has given hope to a generation of weightlifters,
who suddenly see a way out of back-alley
bodybuilding studios.
In a milieu that rewards
rabid McCarthyism
based solely on its rabidity
and ability to exceed
the dementia of a puppet president's
inhuman rhetoric
his movies, every single one of them,
have been remarkably clean
and non-judgmental.
This is a feat
gone unnoticed
for its heroism.
As we have learned
to our pain
all violence is not the same
and to have forged in his scripts
ambiguity

at this point in time
in the stimulus response of Hollywood
in the moral paralysis of jingoistic America
is a deed of epic proportion.

He will never be a Che.
He will never be a Florence Nightingale.
Yet he will also never be paid
to slay Che.
He will move earth to rescue Florence
whether kidnapped by the CIA or the Mafia.
He is, in fact,
what we are missing
to win.

LEFT OUT

It would be a hell of a thing
if, despite monopolies
on television stations
radio stations
satellites
weapons plants
subsidiary weapons plants here in Canada
nuclear reactors
Redeye computer-controlled
and infallible surface-to-air
missiles
Minuteman missiles
Trident missiles
submarines
the forest products industry
offshore oil

the plants that make the trucks that carry
the missiles
24 hours a day seven days a week
around the midwest
demonstration elections
a pride of puppet Latin armies
the cement industry
the mafia
MCA which comprises most
of the movie industry
which has just bought up
three more publishers
the CIA
food-stamp control
oodles of land
on which to build
hidden concentration camps
and a trillion-dollar deficit

if, despite all this
on the other side,
the left had Arnold.

Even one Arnold, a small Arnold
would suffice
to sway the hearts and minds
of us poor villagers.

Imagine:
Arnold at a coalition meeting,
standing and saying "bullshit to this,
let's do it."
Arnold lifting Mulroney
by the feet until he confesses

"Yes, yes, okay, they bought the country from me,
okay okay, let me down,"
and Arnie handing him a pistol—
"Resign or be prosecuted."

Think of the power of one small Arnold
on the picket line outside General Motors
or, *mirabile dictu,*
protesting Star Wars.

Think of a media accountability committee
headed by Arnold.

Think of Arnold
as your father.

THE PERFECT RESUMÉ

Arnold has never made a movie about invading Grenada.
Arnold does not hate Nicaragua.
Arnold has been both a robot assassin
and victor over an alien assassin
that did not differentiate between left and right.
Arnold has never once blown away a woman, bad or good.
He has the power to sculpt his body
into numerous forms.
Arnold never stool-pigeoned for the McCarthy witch hunt,
has never sold used cars,
and has never asked for a single dollar to help God out
of a jam.
He has never flown cocaine into the U.S.
for the CIA
and never said he hated Iran

while selling them missiles.
Arnold has never bombed Libya.
He has never fought commies
who somehow invaded Colorado
nor Soviet assault troops
in the streets of Miami and backroad Georgia.

He has never had to say "I forgot to remember,"
or "I am not a crook,"
and never kicked sand
in someone's face
on the beach.

Arnold has married well,
invested in real estate
and takes care of his parents.

His body is his reference.
He is the cleanest man I know.

THE JOHN WAYNE SEAL OF APPROVAL

It is as much the spirit of John Wayne's characters
herding a generation through the war and past McCarthy
that has kept a number of us
out of US concentration camps
for the politically incorrect
as it has been Arnold's movies
that have prevented the wholesale return
of Hollywood to the early '50s

listen pilgrim,
that Arnold,
he's okay.

HOW IT ENDS

Arnold Schwarzenegger closes the small book of poems, setting it carefully on the glass-topped table in his lucid and beautiful sunroom. Like metallic flares, his eyes close slightly as he looks out beyond the terrace and toward the cold northern clime of Canada, foreign and mysterious.

"You're wrong, my friend," he whispers.

Walking into his bedroom, past the bed on which he will leave a one-word note for Maria, "Canada," he grasps the double closet doors in both powerful hands, pulls them open, and walks into a room about the size of a hardware store. Pulling down from the wall one of several oversize duffle bags, he begins methodically, quickly, with extreme knowledge, to choose weapons, explosives, arms, daggers, shortswords, a halberd, several sawed-off shotguns (pump and auto), a flamethrower, the Smith and Wesson (at this he chuckles), and smaller packages of unexplained ambiguity that might contain C4 explosive.

Passing back through the closet, he chooses a flak jacket, several sleeveless bush vests, and a ripaway t-shirt from his last movie.

A small bottle of the world's most expensive body oil.

His jaw hardens as he listens to the ticket agent on the phone.

"Never mind ... I'll walk." He hangs up.

His oversize hiking boots make no impression in the earth. After a day, he pulls out a field map with a small circle near the top.

In Toronto, I pull the cassette from the VCR. "But did he like this book or not?" I ask myself. There is a short, sharp knock on the door.

The Big House

1

At ten o'clock every morning we start writing in the big house. Sitting with my window open, I hear the various sounds of people at work: typewriter keys being struck at various speeds, the scratch of pens, the thoroughly eradicable whisper of erasers. Here any method of writing is acceptable, encouraged. I choose to ground each blank sheet between *The Complete Posthumous Poems of César Vallejo* and *The Collected Books of Jack Spicer*, then to roll each one singly through an old Underwood "Scriptor" and allow the keys to make their own marks. I must watch closely though. The typewriter likes to write about typing because that is what it does and knows best. Like a negative shepherd, I must watch for evidence of this tendency to remain in the fold's safety, and cut the umbilicus of self-referentiality. I must force the keys to move outward and to expand their horizon through fear. My happiest times here have been when I can rest, and visit my neighbours, with the flock out there somewhere unknown, unseeable, only a few strays left within the bounds of safety.

Here in the big house our goal is to forget ourselves, while remembering all else.

2

William Blake

William Blake is in the room at the farthest end of the corridor from me, nearest the west, by the water, and beside the staircase down to the bar. Hence I do not visit him as often as some of my other neighbours in the big house. I do enjoy his company, though, because he is a short round man like I am, who is seen by all as an eccentric but not without a solid ground connection to the daily life of the house. He carries on an affair with the cook in the kitchen. He keeps close watch on the comings and goings, the internal politics of the big house. I have discussed with him in previous visits my theory that he is really writing about what he sees going on around him in the house, though he changes the names to protect our feelings. He denies any urge to protect feelings. He cites visions to confirm his claim. He hands me today a manuscript page with only a few lines, and I know he is happy in his own way to have a visitor. While I read the few lines, he slices bread warm from the oven in the kitchen.

"Dear chubby William," I say, "you have such an imagination. Though I know there are strangenesses here beyond me, I wonder about the split vision that you have. What does this really mean?"

Smiling, handing me a slice of fresh bread that never seems to fill me up, he explains that there is no imagination involved in the least. "It is really quite simple. I was coming up from the bar last night. There were two angels at the top of the stair. I have only written what I see. That is all."

I cannot argue with him. He is too sweet and lovable and cuddly. I want so much to believe him. I envy him for the room he has. It is so near to the heart of the house—the kitchen.

3

Borges

Borges is right next to me. There is an interconnecting door that we keep locked from either side by mutual agreement. Borges is actually twins, though there are few in the big house who know. They sleep together in the room nearest mine, in twin beds. One is blind, this is true. The reason the other twin is not known is very simple—he has been confined to bed since birth, since he sees everything with startlingly clear blue eyes, but is thoroughly paralyzed, trapped in his body, which is heavy and still like cement.

Like most other twins, the Borges are telepathic to an extreme degree. Yet I confess to having listened through the wall to them talk many times. They are aware I am a voyeur, and perhaps encourage it by their dialogue. Whenever I visit them my throat tickles—their room is full of a dry, dry dust that is breathed out by the large library of old books they have assembled here in the big house. The piles of books are inexhaustible. I do not know if they can speak all the languages, I suspect they can speak only their own, and yet this allows access to all. The dust collects in my throat after a time there, but after the cough I do not mind being infected.

Jorge insists on paying for an entire suite of rooms in the big house, though as far as I can tell they have only the one.

4

Bill Burroughs

I first met Burroughs when I went down the hall to complain about the jazz keeping me awake at the ungodly hour. He came to the door in his rumpled grey suit with a string tie loosely cinched about his neck.

"They all just left," he said. "Spicer, Kerouac, Ginsberg, Cassady. You're just a bit too late." I recognized his twang as the one I heard scat-singing for what seemed an eternity. I found myself explaining that I had certain preconceptions of age, including quietness, and a desire to put things together, rather than tear them down. I thought that riotous behaviour might endanger the big house and whatever it was meant to achieve. He explained that most slept right through the night, that though our rooms are connected by the halls, they are actually quite separate.

We talked for hours about choice.

I have come to believe that if a starship ever lands outside the big house, by the water of the lake, where I have often imagined it to happen, Bill will be chosen by some means to communicate. In many ways we have agreed we are opposites, and thus always try to attend the same functions in the big house, though often on far sides of the same crowd.

1968

Three flowers of blood appear on Rudi—
one on his head, a blood rose
through his throat, a bird flying
in the chest, one bouquet of coral.

How to fall down.
So easy.

In my stomach
the scale model of Buchenwald.
Yum.
Lit by the firebombed Dresden
of my heart.
How cosy.

He dies, yes—that is,
he was transformed
into nothing
through a leakage of the body.
That's all, folks.

A shower, a bath
alters surface charge
on the skin.

Humans Equal Angels After Death Pope Says

For Cris Cuddy

Humans equal angels after death pope says &
The word is a virus burroughs says &
We have to take a stand somewhere reagan says &
What do you do with a lonesome gorilla cris sings &
I have seen the best minds of my generation ginsberg says &
Dreams are after all just dreams first of all

I am innocent of all crimes I didn't know I committed I say &
Humans equal viral angels because somebody has to
Reagan says to burroughs in the stadium in Argentina
It's a living isn't it &
Gorillas don't say anything at all do they
Do they
I said

Add Language

Language has crawled on its hands and knees to be here

Buddy can you help language out
Language has had its toenails pulled out in south american prisons
Language fills you up not out
Language cannot hear you it has a banana in its ear
Language will save you
This language has been drilled in the mysteries at Fort Bragg
And dropped on several countries at night to infiltrate the political
  system
Language has a tiger in its tank
Every Friday night for years language has gotten together and
  gotten drunk
Then torn through town giving decent citizens a black eye
Language races faster without the blinkers on
Language should be led past certain things with blinkers on
Language is blinkers
It has been left out in the rain and has warped
Before the discovery of language men travelled in horse-drawn grunts
Language is progress
And infinity
And limitation
Language is the mote in the eye of the god
Who wears blinkers
Moreover, language gives you more miles per gallon
And two chances to win, not just one
Language is the taste of lemon meringue pie
And finely ground pepper rubbed in fresh cuts
And shit
Whosoever finds language he shall be a lucky man
Language is woman
Language is the flag they raised on a hill on Iwo Jima
Language is a coon, a spic, a wop, a kike, a kaffir, a wasp
Has starred in movies as Stepinfetchit, Cool Hand Luke, Barbarella,

Mickey Mouse, Joan of Arc, Heathcliff, Sherlock Holmes
Coming soon as Ronald Reagan, Idi Amin, Frank Zappa and Sara
the Chimp
Read the book of language—
Soon to be a major screenplay
Buy the language doll
Language is the secret code which when broken heals itself
Language is the cure for cancer
Speak to me only with thine language
To be in the desert with a loaf, a jug of wine and language
Two languages are better than one
Language is what distinguishes us from the angels
It will keep its head while all around they are losing theirs
It will improve your game
Care for the wife and kids
Language is the best chance for career advancement
Language is the true way and the path, the *tao*
And it is absolutely nowhere
Never was, never will be
Language is a hot number, a box lunch, an easy piece of tail,
a dyke, a queer, an odd duck, a bad business, a sad end
Language is better than a kick in the ass

More impersonal than a gold watch

All that is left of the lost continent of Atlantis
Language is something coming in under the radar sir
We can't trace it
Language is a neutron bomb that has always just gone off
It is better to light one candle than to curse the language
Language is the freedom to misquote all that has not been said forever.

And When the Kid Drowned on My Mother It Became an Angel

It slid beneath the wave
of breathing, it wasn't living was
it when they found it? At that precise
release a thousand miniature angels
in their disguise as a pale child
burst through the sand
surrounding my mother
who cried but the child
is drowning
and with a fiery sword
the precise angel of beauty
cleaved her breath from her chest
and she fell down
into hell.

The lifeguard
struggled against a current
of cries
and pulled something white
from the last dregs of clean water
ever to flow through Kingston
and tumbled it onto the beach
amid the thousand misbegotten
doubts.

In that last shudder
of gilled lungs
this childish manta
bellied forth
what else?
My mother and any number
of sad children
wondering where that previous world
had sunk.

The Grand Tour

For Jesse Mackew

Princess Street arcs north then curves like a stream of urine from
a full bladder.
This is the Kingston of my dreams. It sits like a cigarette burn
On a map, like a congealed French fry at the side of the road, like
A kidney stone blocking a tube.

Look—there's Alfred Street where some cruel ass told me I'd be arrested
If I put my hands on the guy wire of a telephone pole, where if I'd known
Just down the hill the pound sat trembling behind a fence, I could have
signed myself in
And hoped for adoption or euthanasia.

Look—there is Division Street where Lino's used to be, where acid
made the hoods
Less Italian, where Neil threw me over the hood of a car
Briefly, there were rats there were waitresses who would feign affection
Till you took a cab home with them at 3 a.m. and yet they always went
upstairs alone

Look—there is a hospital, a university, a library, a Chinese restaurant,
a sculpture,
The shoes of Ariel Dorfman, a train held captive in a park. All the trappings
That Kingston uses to try and pass for normal. It is not normal.
It is Kingston. A cyst of memory on the lake, a ripped-out toenail of despair.

Imagine—there's the corner where my brother died.
The streetlight outside his (former) window says get over it, you've
got others.

Kim wrote me a sestina in which he explained everything but
It got lost in the mail. I still hope it will arrive.

I have made an enemy of the Tourist Bureau.
I was threatened with a punch on the nose by the Parks Commissioner.
The City Council banned me from the building.
I was scared to leave because I'd never been anywhere else.

1957

You take three loose bullets from the glove compartment.
It is 1957.
You are hot & sweaty & already not very tall.
They are little spaceships you could escape in.
You show them to your brother Kim.
You show them to your sister Jane.
There are some really nice rocks
You've often run your hand over
On the edge of the road.
Hey lookit this you say.
You put a bullet on the rock.
You hit it with a rock.
It bangs.
You fall over
But no one sees.
Kim takes a rock
And hits a bullet.
There is a bang.
Jane takes a rock
And copies Kim.
There is a bang.
They walk over to see what else is in the glove compartment.
You lie there
Absorbing radiation.

Gird Thine Loins

No particular Wednesday they chased me up the tree by throwing firecrackers. I climbed up till I saw the planets & the stars revolving on circles round the sun & my lungs emptied into a spray of crystals & I fell till I was old.

Proposals

I

Alter human beings
To suit extant
Technology.

By insertion
Of several gears
Into the jaw
& a ratchet in the heart.

Suffering can be
Conquered.

II

Move mountains
Into the ocean.

This way men
Can walk
To Europe
Over the Atlantic.

All it will take
Is time.

III

Give people the means
To talk more.
Fill the world up

With sound,
Long-distance calls
And aeroplanes.

They will find themselves
At peace.

Performance: The Disappeared Ones

PLACE BOOK STANDING ON TABLE
Where were you?
KNOCK BOOK TO FLOOR WITH FIST
Where do you spend the night?
KICK IT FORWARD
Do you have anything to hide?
STAMP ON IT WITH FOOT
Is this a fish or a scar?
PUNCH BOOK IN FACE
What kind of car did you use?
PUNCH BOOK AGAIN HARDER
Can you feel this?
PLUNGE KNIFE INTO BOOK LYING ON FLOOR
Do you feel discouraged about the future?
BREAK SPINE OF BOOK
Do you feel more ugly than you used to?
RIP COVER OFF BOOK
How is your appetite?
TEAR PAGES OUT BY HAND
Have you ever been in trouble about your sex behaviour?
SPIT ON BOOK
Does your head hurt?
KNEEL ON BOOK WITH HAMMER IN HAND RAISED
Have you lived the right kind of life?
POUND PAGES WITH HAMMER
Do you tease animals?
BITE PAGES OUT WILDLY WITH TEETH
Are you easily downed in an argument?
THROW BOOK TO FLOOR
Do you believe in law enforcement?
JUMP UP AND DOWN ON IT
Have you ever vomited blood or coughed up blood?
BURN WITH CIGARETTE
Do you keep a diary?

THROW BOOK INTO AIR
Are you afraid to handle money?
ON KNEES, STROKE THEN SLAP BOOK
Is there something wrong with your mind?
LIGHT BOOK WITH MATCH
Is it true that everything tastes the same?
PUT FIRE OUT WITH HAND
Are there among your acquaintances any carpenters?
RELIGHT IT
How much water do you drink in a day?
POUR WATER FROM GLASS ONTO BOOK
Do you wish you were dead?
LIFT BOOK UP THEN SLAM TO FLOOR
Give up?
SMASH WATER GLASS ON BOOK
Do you have any political opinions?
SET BOOK BACK ON TABLE

Salvador

driving west a
cross Ontario I saw
two soldiers walk into a room filled
with your blood, your
corpse, backed
away

raised weapons, pointing
at you, there was a sound &
smoke & their guns
caused your blood to soften
to run into holes &
missing parts of your body
return until they had drunk their fill
& then sucking a small metal lump from
your body caused
the holes to close, your body to
upright itself in a random series of obscene
twitches & stand, your eyes
newly covered by your glasses which
levitated from the floor to your face

unthankful you peered at them
defiantly, the fervour of your regard
caused them to step backward through doors that slammed shut
on their world

I Bought a Hat in Spain

Who's against poetry
But a humid businessman named Artaud?
A priest lacking one thing?
A general who doubts the miasma?
A vagabond who pisses on everything
Including the very visage of death?
Someone who talks bad to you?
A dancer on the precipice
of a narcissist, ya gotta love that!
Bloody joker, but
Deliberately miserable?
How about a poet who lives in a missile silo,
An alchemist of these times?
A plastic-bagged revolutionary,
Bringing home the tasty little bourgeoisies?
A nut?
Some god, the innocent!
Or maybe some petty little alderman from a shipping town?
Underline your answer!

What is it that poetry has against itself:
Temporal tea?
A rock sliced by snow?
Maybe a wallet full of human poop?
God thinks so.
A spy telling the truth?
A news flash from your face
Direct to a writer of your own?
Hold your horses—
Some cheap pass at young poets?
Artaud eating a sausage?
Then flying apart because

Artaud is full of gas?
Some thin artery about to explode?
Take note of the Cross
Which many consider correct.

After "Test" by Nicanor Parra

Whose Dog Is You

After Alexander Pope

Whose dog is you?
Whose hand was bit?
Where from does you run?
Where to?

What is this collar of thorns?

50 Thanks No Particular Order!

Thanks Samuel Beckett for the pencils!
Thanks Ho Chi Minh for the map!
Thanks Judy Merril for the black eye!
Thanks John Fyles for the t-shirt.
Thanks Kim Smith for the key ring!
Thanks Vladimir Mayakovsky for the haircut!
Thanks bpNichol for the game!
Thanks Henry Miller for the words!
Thanks Misha for the skip!
Thanks U Thant for flying!
Thanks Augusto Sandino for dying!
Thanks Georges Boulogne for the duel!
Thanks Le Comte d'Eon for the dress!
Thanks Jones for the tabloid!
Thanks Thea Riley for one kiss!
Thanks Jim Morrison for the blood!
Thanks Laura Nyro for your voice!
Thanks Steve McQueen for the blink!
Thanks Ella Margaret Smith for the photo!
Thanks Stan Rogers for the baldness!
Thanks Ezra Pound for the gold!
Thanks Tim Leary for the laugh track!
Thanks Arnie for the licks!
Thanks William Burroughs for the wild!
Thanks Enrique Lihn for harsh words!
Thanks Roque Dalton for escaping!
Thanks Arthur Sohn for sleeping!
Thanks Ila Annan for the song!
Thanks Leonel Rugama for the bank job!
Thanks Allen Ginsberg for offending!
Thanks Jean Genet for the shipmate!
Thanks Harry Annan for the gamble!
Thanks Arthur Rimbaud for the guns!
Thanks Joe Strummer for living!

Thanks Alexander Bell for fear of moonlight!
Thanks John Kennedy for the Catholic!
Thanks Victor Jara for little houses!
Thanks Johnny Horton for the Bismarck!
Thanks Pierre Trudeau for being hated!
Thanks Louis Dudek for the letters!
Thanks Blackie for exploding!
Thanks Cleo for the fish!
Thanks Richard Swanton for the teddy bear!
Thanks Robert Heinlein for the sex!
Thanks Tristan Tzara for zigzags!
Thanks Dan Harrison for one beer!
Thanks Salvador for the army!
Thanks Pablo Neruda for Isla Negra!
Thanks Salvador Allende for the glasses!
Thanks Man Ray for the hat!
Thanks
Thanks
Thanks

Notes on Some of the Poems

Assassin Take One: Gene Day was a Gananoque underground cartoonist who had just made it big with Marvel when he had a massive stroke. Arnie was my dog from 1988 to 2003. bp was, as McFadden says, the late great bpNichol.

Crinoid Hill: A poem about driving, fossil hunting and a baby in a blue blanket.

Your Big Day: One of my fondest wishes is for Nicanor Parra to read this.

A Final Vision: The vegetables here were grown from Robert Kroetsch's lovely 1977 book, *Seed Catalogue.*

To Roque Dalton in El Salvador—Letter One: The brilliant Salvadoran communist writer Roque Dalton lived from 1935 to 1975, wrote over a dozen books, escaped the death penalty by climbing out of his cell after an earthquake and was assassinated by members of his own revolutionary party. Please seek out *Poemas Clandestinos,* available in a bilingual edition from Curbstone Press.

Ombra Completa: A Translation from Sleep: My only homage to Chilean singer Victor Jara—so far.

The Freak Brothers: One of several pieces done in contemplation of a little-known German revolutionary group led by working-class hero Bommi Baumann, author of *Wie es alles anfing* (*How It All Began*).

Ike Met Space Aliens: I still have a fading cassette of the broadcast comedy tape of this from U of T's then-fledgling CIUT around 1983. It is as accurate an account of the period as any other.

Mayakovsky: Kim, also mentioned in the opening poem of this collection, was the oldest of my younger brothers. He was a gentle, lovely person who lived too short a time. The Russian poet Vladimir Mayakovsky lived an even shorter time, earlier. I wish they had both lived long enough to meet.

Forgot to Tell You: The Spanish phrase *hay peligro, tonto,* means *it's dangerous, stupid!*

13/4/83: Partial appropriation of the voice of an imagined West German revolutionary.

VIRUS: At a writers' retreat north of Bracebridge, an ungodly dog howl caused me to peer out the window into the dark, just as a scrap of birch bark crawled along the roof.

To Leonel Rugama in Nicaragua—Letter Two: Leonel Rugama of Nicaragua got shot dead at 20 freeing up cash from a bank for the Sandinista cause. He never saw the success of the revolution, nor his first and only book of astonishing poetry, published posthumously. I trace my early interest in Nicaragua to having seen the coverage of the long siege laid to the bank by the National Guard that ended in Leonel's death.

Message Remnant: Originally dictated through an old-style black rotary phone.

Lachrymose: Back to Managua. The Mercado Oriental is the main marketplace. *Presente* is defined in the poem.

I Am Amazed: My only true socialist realist work.

After Vallejo's This/Happened Between Two: César Vallejo, Peruvian poet, died at 45 in '38. His *Spain, Take This Cup from Me* is required reading for entry into heaven.

The Toll: Alexander Graham Bell had a very, very strong fear of moonlight. He would go to great lengths to ensure it did not shine on his loved ones while they slept.

Don't Forget Alberti: The porcine mound of maggot shit is of course Generalissimo Franco, of whom the world was finally relieved in 1975, allowing Alberti to return from his lifetime of exile.

One Thousand Nine Hundred Thirty Words: It would have been nice to meet Nicanor Parra. Still theoretically possible, but with him 95, I better get crackin'.

The Cuban Missile Crisis: We moved every six months or so throughout most of the '60s. I spent October '62 at a Catholic school in the north of Kingston. My only surviving memory is of me standing out in the yard by some bleachers, staring up into the sky at recess and lunch, scared as hell of the warheads I knew were about to rain down.

No Pasarán: Means *they shall not pass.*

The Morning Before High Noon: Another goodbye to Gene Day, who ran the Haunted House in Gananoque with his wife, Gale Jack.

Prayer: Presumptively written on the day they killed Roque Dalton.

Campo de Batalla: The Chilean painter Eugenio Tellez is one of my favourite people. He is one of my favourite painters. He is a friend of our friend George Manupelli, who founded the Ann Arbor Film Festival. He and the painter Mindy Camponeschi, one of my favourite human beings on this planet, used to be married. *Campo de Batalla* means *Field of Battle* and was the title of one of Eugenio's shows in Chile.

Street Survival: This found its beginnings in *Soldier of Fortune* magazine.

The Schwarzenegger Poems: Written in a heated week of hero-longing at Saskatchewan Writers Guild's Fort San Retreat in '88. Sent it to him, but got no response.

1968: A remnant of an examination of a revolutionary working-class group in Germany.

And When the Kid Drowned on My Mother It Became an Angel: Sadly based on a real event.

The Grand Tour: After 32 years away, I still harbour feelings about Kingston.

1957: Out past the oil tanks, in the country, way past Cataraqui. Near the sales barn, near the 4-room school where I did grades 1-4 in 3 years in 2 rooms. Near where Blackie the dog got killed. The first U.S. underground nuclear test took place on September 19 in Nevada.

I Bought a Hat in Spain: Thanks to you, Nicanor!

Acknowledgements

The Selected Poems have previously appeared in various books and magazines, occasionally in slightly different form.

"Les Anges du Péché" and "I Am Amazed" appeared in *Surface Structures* (St. Lawrence College/Kingston Writers Association, 1979).

"Anger," "13/4/83," "The Freak Brothers," "Mayakovsky," "One Hundred Most Frightening Things," "Why I Am Such a Nice Guy," and "1968" appeared in *One Hundred Most Frightening Things* (blewointmentpress, 1985).

"Ombra Completa: A Translation from Sleep," "After Vallejo's This/Happened Between Two," "After Vallejo's Well Does the Pallid Metalloid Heal You?," "After Parra's Self-Portrait," "Street Survival," "The Finger," "John," and "The Big House" appeared in *Convincing Americans* (Proper Tales Press, 1986).

"A Final Vision," "Message Remnant," "The Toll," "Song of the Caller," and "Proposals" appeared in *Translating Sleep* (Wolsak and Wynn, 1989).

"To Roque Dalton in El Salvador—Letter One," "The Little Bird," "South," "To Leonel Rugama in Nicaragua—Letter Two," "Lachrymose," "Investigative Loss," "The Corpse," "This Just In" (as "Then If"), and "Prayer" appeared in *Leonel/Roque* (Coteau Books, 1998).

"Crinoid Hill" appeared in a chapbook of the same name (The Front Press, 1986); likewise "VIRUS" (Underwhich Editions, 1983); "The Schwarzenegger Poems" (Surrealist Poets' Gardening Assoc., 1988); and "TELEGRAMS" (Proper Tales Press Blind Date, 1988).

"Ike Met Space Aliens" appeared in the tabloid *The Goblin*; "On the Breaking of Discipline," "Performance: The Disappeared Ones," and "Declarations of War" in *This Magazine*; "Coda" in *Who Torched Rancho Diablo?*, "The Morning Before High Noon" in *Eat Me, Literally*, "Playing Golf with the Colonels" in *Piranha*, "Humans Equal Angels After Death Pope Says" in *Acta Victoriana*, "Ledger Entry" and "And When the Kid Drowned on My Mother It Became an Angel" in *Poetry Toronto*.

"Add Language" appeared in the anthology *The Inner Ear* (Cormorant Books, 1982).

The author thanks the editors of these publications.

The poems not cited above are the New Poems.

OTHER BOOKS BY THE AUTHOR

Surface Structures (St. Lawrence College/Kingston Writers Association, 1979)
Virus (Underwhich Editions, 1983)
One Hundred Most Frightening Things (blewointmentpress, 1985)
Convincing Americans (Proper Tales Press, 1986)
Crinoid Hill (The Front Press, 1986)
The Schwarzenegger Poems (Surrealist Poets' Gardening Assoc., 1988)
Telegrams (Proper Tales Press Blind Date, 1988)
Translating Sleep (Wolsak and Wynn, 1989)
Head Cutter (The Front Press Manuscript Editions, 1992)
Seven Pieces of Dream for Nora Astorga (The Front Press Manuscript Editions, 1992)
Daddee (The Front Press Manuscript Editions, 1993)
Sandino for Kids (The Front Press Manuscript Editions, 1993)
Leonel/Roque (Coteau Books, 1998)

Jim Smith moved from his birthplace, Niagara Falls, to Kingston in 1952. He started writing seriously in Grade 8 in 1963. His first published story earned him $5 from *West Coast Review* in 1972. His magazine, *The Front*, lasted from about 1972 to 1980, and the spinoff Front Press published books and pamphlets in the '80s by writers like David McFadden, bpNichol, Lillian Necakov, Wayne Clifford and Stuart Ross. Between 1979 and 1998, Smith published about half a dozen books of poetry, plus a number of chapbooks and ephemera. In the mid-'90s he diverted himself to law, and has been a civil litigator for the last decade. He continues to live and write in Toronto.

BOOKS FROM MANSFIELD PRESS

Poetry

Leanne Averbach, *Fever*
Diana Fitzgerald Bryden, *Learning Russian*
Alice Burdick, *Flutter*
Margaret Christakos, *wipe.under.a.love*
Pino Coluccio, *First Comes Love*
Gary Michael Dault, *The Milk of Birds*
Pier Giorgio Di Cicco, *Early Works*
Pier Giorgio Di Cicco, *The Visible World*
Christopher Doda, *Aesthetics Lesson*
Rishma Dunlop, *Metropolis*
Ollivier Dyens, *The Profane Earth*
Suzanne Hancock, *Another Name for Bridge*
Jason Heroux, *Emergency Hallelujah*
Jason Heroux, *Memoirs of an Alias*
Carole Glasser Langille, *Late in a Slow Time*
Jeanette Lynes, *The Aging Cheerleader's Alphabet*
David W. McFadden, *Be Calm, Honey*
Lillian Necakov, *The Bone Broker*
Catherine Owen & Joe Rosenblatt, with Karen Moe, *Dog*
Corrado Paina, *The Alphabet of the Traveler*
Corrado Paina, *Souls in Plain Clothes*
Jim Smith, *Back Off, Assassin! New & Selected Poems*
Robert Earl Stewart, *Something Burned Along the Southern Border*
Steve Venright, *Floors of Enduring Beauty*
Brian Wickers, *Stations of the Lost*

Fiction

Kent Nussey, *A Love Supreme*
Kent Nussey, ed., *Particle & Wave*
Tom Walmsley, *Dog Eat Rat*

Non-fiction

Pier Giorgio Di Cicco, *Municipal Mind*
Amy Lavender Harris, *Imagining Toronto*